Foreword

By Bill Tacchella

(Husband of the Author)

In Christ, there is always hope, even in tough times. Often, the fruit of difficult situations is that we experience our most significant changes and notable personal growth. The book of James starts with an incredible promise, *"Consider it all joy, my brethren, when you encounter various trials, knowing that the testing of your faith produces endurance. And let endurance have its perfect result, so that you may be perfect and complete, lacking in nothing. But if any of you lacks wisdom, let him ask of God, who gives to all generously and without reproach, and it will be given to him"* (James 1:2-5). With the demise of my mother-in-law, we asked, expected, and received God's wisdom at every curve along the road.

This is the story of my wife's journey with her mother through her final years of Alzheimer's. I always teased Betsy's mother that she was my favorite mother-in- law. Of course, she was the only one, but what a delightful, energetic, elegant, and beautiful lady she was. We had a warm and wonderful relationship which makes the loss defined in this story all the more difficult. However, this account is also one of triumph. Yes, there were tears along the way, but it was more a time of hope, encouragement, and experiencing God in fresh ways.

Although it's hard sometimes to find blessings in the midst of dementia such as Alzheimer's, my best remembrance of Doris Dixon Brown was that she was such a vibrant woman. Even in the final stages of Alzheimer's, although lost in a new and often terrifying world, she was still my favorite mother-in-law.

My wife had decided that she would consider this season as a journey in faith, trusting that Jesus Christ would travel with them, providing the strength and grace needed to make the load lighter and more bearable. This kind of trek is never an easy one. Along the way, it appeared at times that there was no hope, that the loss was unbearable, but with Christ there was always a path through. His light led the way. His grace was indeed sufficient and His power evident for both of them. It was as though God had given my wife a checkbook of grace, and there were always "sufficient funds" available (II Cor. 12:9).

Whereas Alzheimer's is incurable and the loss is both mental and physical, it is possible to maintain dignity and comfort. Doris was loved to the end. Her demise proved that faith was triumphant. As a family, we learned what Alzheimer's is, and we learned valuable lessons in faith, courage, love and servant-hood. You will find this to be a sweet story.

Several years later, we started again on the same journey with my father. We will never regret honoring our parents. We trust that this is part of the legacy that we will leave our children and grandchildren, as our parents left one for us. God bless you as you read this book. It has left our family with tears, laughter, and joy at God's provision for us.

1
The Time Had Come

It's difficult to know when it started. Alzheimer's comes on so slowly at first. It's the little things that all of us wonder about as we age. *Was that a senior moment? I seem to be remembering less, sometimes forgetting a name or unable to bring up a word. Could this mean...?* These were the kinds of questions that percolated in my mind concerning my mother. There were just too many peculiar incidents occurring too regularly and now with alarming increase. What options did I need to consider? Choices were facing me, the kind we all hope to put off with an aging parent, yet for many of us, become a necessary part of life. As a daughter, I was about to embark on an interesting, if not remarkable, and lengthy journey. It began with a plane ride.

I couldn't put off the difficult decision any longer. The time had come to move Mother. With twinges of anxiety, unsure of what I would encounter or what to expect, I boarded a plane to Arizona. Butterflies bounced around in my stomach, and my heart hammered as I blew a wisp of hair from my forehead. Drawing a deep breath, I headed down the narrow aisle of the plane. After hefting my carry-on into the overhead compartment, I collapsed into my assigned seat and let out an audible sigh. Securing my seatbelt, I leaned back, closed my eyes and drifted into imaginations of what awaited me in Arizona.

Quickly lost in my thoughts, I was thankful traveling from Michigan to Arizona would allow me time to process and reflect on Mother's strange behavior and the task that lay before me. Questions loomed and swirled in my mind. *What would my week in Arizona hold? What new changes would I observe in Mother? What in the world could be wrong with her anyway?* My mind played out various scenarios of what lay ahead. A bit restless, I contemplated that nothing made sense. Her recent behavior did not fit in a black and white box. I hate the unknown and clearly, I was moving into what felt like a dense, lingering fog, dark and unapproachable. I'm an upfront sort of person who likes to be in control of situations. This situation was definitely out of my comfort zone.

Slipping back from my contemplation, out of the corner of my eye I observed a slightly plump, gray haired lady settling into the seat next to me. Giving her a polite smile, I couldn't help but notice the jovial look on her face. "Hello," she offered. "Are you headed home? By the way, I'm Martha."

"No," I replied. "I'm headed to Arizona to visit my mother."

Would I have to talk to Martha? She looked like the talkative type. Part of me just wanted to retreat into my own world, alone with my thoughts, to continue pondering various scenarios and expectations which surely awaited me on the other side of this flight. But then, I remembered what I had recently prayed....

Soon the plane crept back from its assigned slot. The wearying announcements were made by flight attendants who were probably just as eager as the passengers to take off. We taxied down the runway and were smoothly airborne. As my fingers gripped the arms of the seat, I watched the earth below as it diminished in size. I wondered if my tension was due to the upward movement of the plane or the situation I would soon be plunged into.

Glancing out the window, I noticed the sky looked so peaceful...every puffy cloud in place, a reminder that the God of the universe would be my constant companion on this trip. Events unknown to me were securely known by Him. I felt reassured and consoled with that thought as I began to ponder the things that led up to the difficult decision to move Mother.

Mother had lived in her home in Arizona for fifteen years. It was a comfortable, modest, single story home on a quiet street in Mesa. She loved lots of light in her home so, of course, open drapes, sunshine, and a cheery atmosphere greeted every guest.

Unlike our lush green Michigan yard, hers was typical of Arizona, consisting of rocks and desert plants. Certainly easier to maintain.

My father, Ralph, a kind hearted, gray haired man had died in 1974, so she lived alone. His demise had been a grueling time for her. Since I lived so far away, care during his last days fell to my mother and Delores, a visiting nurse. Mother had cajoled my father for two years to see a doctor, but he would have none of it. With the specific symptoms he had, I think he knew he had cancer and was scared to death to hear that frightening word. The thought of chemo and radiation treatments had paralyzed him into inaction. By the time we finally got him to go in for a check up, it was as he had feared. Surgery was scheduled immediately. The surgeon opened him up, took one look, sewed him back up, and sent him home. "It's too late," the surgeon sternly barked to my mother as he met with her in the hallway of the hospital. I thought she would collapse from the jolt of his pungent, insensitive words spoken with no bedside manner at all.

It was a grueling moment, followed by months of anguish. He died at home after six months of excruciating pain. It was an awful time for both of them. But my mother is Pollyanna personified and, as I could have predicted, she eventually bounced back. Perhaps she felt relieved that her agony had also passed.

No one can really know another's pain and suffering. We each have our own burdens in life. We can empathize with others, but there are also things we are called to go through that we alone carry. Galatians 6:2 says, *"Bear one another's burdens, and thereby fulfill the law of Christ,"* a reminder that we can pray for and lift others up. But Galatians 6:5 quickly follows with, *"For each one will bear his own load."* There are dark times when only those who are experiencing the pain can understand. I think my father's demise was one of those times for Mother.

After a time of grieving my father's death, Mother eventually learned to be content with her independent life. Adjustments came with living alone, but she never complained. Always seeing the bright side of any new situa-tion, to her the proverbial glass was always half full, and she likened each new day to a happy adventure. Mother again returned to her normal social routine.

After our father's death, my younger sister and only sibling, Cynthia, and I had urged Mother to move to a retirement home to relieve the burden of the many responsibilities that go with maintaining a house. No, no, no! She would have none of that, and who could blame her. Who wants to leave the comfort and security of familiarity? I'm sure that idea sounded ominous and threatening. Even the thought made her feel disconnected, cold, distant, and certainly afraid.

Would a new place be sunny and well lighted like her house? Would her furniture fit? Would it feel like home? What about neighbors? With her brother, Don, and his wife, Betty, living just a block away, she felt a closeness and security that couldn't be replaced. On her daily walks, she frequently passed by their home, waving a cheery hello or just noticing whether their drapes were open for the day. It was an anchor in her life to know they were close by.

Cynthia and I had so hoped to find solace and a sense of relief in knowing that Mother was in a retirement home where she could still remain independent yet have fewer demands and responsibilities in her life. A place where staff would greet her each day and tend to her needs. A place where her meals would be provided, maintenance problems tended to, no lawn or garden to look after, a safe place. But our hopes of her making a choice to move on her own never met with reality. She resisted every suggestion.

As time went on, however, Cynthia and I began to notice some abnormal and unexplainable behavior patterns. With this new conduct, we faced moving her for another, unexpected reason, a reason none of us fully understood, one that seemed oblique and puzzling. We had the unpleasant task of moving her now against her will.

2
Forgetfulness

Mother had always enjoyed an active social life, loving her bridge parties and luncheons. Whenever I visited her home, I always found four or five brightly colored invitations hanging above her phone in the kitchen. "Betty's having a bridge luncheon Friday," she would explain, or "Esther is having a group over for a dinner party tomorrow." Her cheery invitations hung as trophies of her popularity in social circles. Mother had carved out a comfortable niche in her community. Everyone liked her and rightly so. She was even tempered, always looking for the best in people, accepting everyone regardless of their station in life.

I didn't think much about her behavioral changes at first, but in a corner of my mind, I wondered why she suddenly began to back away from her friends and her social activities. With each phone call, I would hear about one more event that she had chosen not to attend. First, she stopped attending bridge parties. We assumed she had just grown tired of bridge after years of being an avid, top notch player. In retrospect, we realized she probably just forgot how to play.

I recall many evenings as a teenager when I would sit at the bridge table alongside my mother, watching her every move, thinking how sharp she was at cards. She seemed to remember every card that was played. Her ability to strategize in this complicated card game spoke of her keen mental acuity.

Another change we noticed was that she spoke less and less about her friends, as though she had cut herself off from almost everyone. Only one or two visited her now, and she herself stopped initiating outings. Several close friends had passed away, but we observed that she seldom saw or visited with others in her large circle of acquaintances. This struck us as odd, since Mother had never lacked for social life. Drawn to her smiling countenance, people enjoyed her sunny personality and positive conversation. One of her friends told me that she had never heard my mother say an unkind word about anyone. To me that sounded super human, but I believed it was true.

Now her life was beginning to seem like a room with a dimmer light fixture that was slowly being turned down, one that in the end makes it hard to distinguish what's in the room. Yes, odd behavior patterns were creeping into her conduct.

At the time we hadn't thought too much about her unusual reports of travel either. She explained on the phone that when she flew now, she ordered a wheelchair and asked a stewardess to wheel her to the next terminal or to the baggage claim. This was odd because Mother loved walking, and she hadn't complained of any physical ailment. True, there had been several occasions when blood clots in her legs had rendered her prone for weeks at a time, but not now. She had bounced back after these episodes and continued her social engagements. Now, her behavior just seemed peculiar.

Mother was an early riser who could be found walking her neighborhood at six o'clock every morning. It was a glorious time of day to her. The secret of survival in the summer in Arizona, she claimed, was to rise early and enjoy the outdoors at sunrise. She loved the Arizona lifestyle. The hot weather suited her just fine. Never mind that steering wheels melted, and dehydration could claim a victim even in a short neighborhood walk in the summer. At 6:00 A.M. the sun had not reached scorching levels yet, so every morning, with an umbrella in hand, she strolled through the neighborhood on a mission to greet as many neighbors as possible. Her cheery hello brought continual smiles in return.

So, for Mother to be riding instead of walking in an airport was totally out of character. What could cause this change in her routine? It wasn't until months later we surmised that perhaps she feared getting lost in the airport. At that time her mind still functioned enough to reason out ways to cope. It's amazing how we humans can compensate for our shortcomings.

It's hard to imagine what must go on in the mind of a person who is gradually losing mental function, especially to the point where their coping skills no longer work for them, where they can't even remember how to manage every day life. What must Mother have been thinking as she moved through the early stages of Alzheimer's? It's hard to know. She never spoke of it.

One of our defense mechanisms as humans is to compensate in order to adapt. For instance, when my husband had a stroke in 2004, he lost his lower left peripheral vision in both eyes. He had to learn to use the mirrors on his car more diligently and turn his head to see if a car was next to him. One of the challenges Mother had, even before Alzheimer's, was a habit of avoiding things that she didn't want to talk about. Now, with her mind tricking her, it would have been very helpful if she had developed a pattern of transparency and openness earlier in life. Perhaps all of us would have benefited and been better able to understand her fears, disorientation, and the mental "lost-ness" that came later.

The mind is an amazing thing. I suppose we all find ways to cope or compensate on some level, depending on our personal shortcomings. For me, one area is map sense. I have been directionally impaired since birth. If you ask whether a well known city is east or west, I have to picture the entire United States in my mind, where I am presently, and where the city is located. Even on a clear day with the sun up, I have to envision a map to discern north from south. And that's on a good day. Usually, I have no idea what direction I'm going. To compensate, I try to surround myself with map proficient people or directions from mapquest.com. I have been lost more times than I can count, and I'm sure there are some gas stations that moan when they see me coming for directions again. It doesn't seem to matter how many times I've been to a particular town, the same scenario of directional confusion manages to repeat itself. I thank God for the invention of GPS! Now, if I can only figure out how to get the address punched in. I digress...

Perhaps, in the beginning stages of Mother's dementia, she felt a similar confusion. Perhaps, all the airport terminals looked the same. We'll never know for sure. We're just thankful she arrived to her destinations safely.

3
Carl

One evening our phone rang. It was Carl, a dear friend of Mother's. A tall, balding, but stately gentleman with a pleasant and proper demeanor, Carl had been Mother's friend for several years. Having spent his adult years in Beatrice, Nebraska, he and his wife had also retired in Arizona. In his late seventies, he lost his wife around the same time my father passed away. Wistfully, he lamented one time, "I'd marry your mother if I were ten years younger." Carl surely did find ways to show his love to Mother. Much of his time was spent tending to her in the early stages of her downward spiral, always keeping us informed as to how she was doing. We were thankful for Carl's kind attention. If it hadn't been for him, Mother couldn't have stayed in Arizona as long as she did.

Carl had debated whether to call us one particular evening but decided it was the prudent thing to do. His voice showed concern as he reported that Mother had stopped cooking and was losing weight. "I'm taking her out to eat several times a week," he explained, "but outside of that, I'm not sure she's eating anything." At first this news alarmed me, but because I lived so far away and had no clue as to the veracity of his report, I decided not to overreact. Instead, I simply phoned Mother who assured me that, of course, she was eating enough.

Without knowing the scope of her confusion, I believed her and thought Carl must be mistaken. I look back at this time with sadness in my heart. How could I have missed such an obvious symptom? But I had always trusted Mother, and if she felt she was eating enough, I thought Carl must be over reacting. Probably all adult children want to believe their parents are capable and trustworthy. After all, they're our parents. In reality, my ignorance of Alzheimer's disease was causing me to under-react.

I guess everyone has regrets in life. Even today I look back and feel a certain remorse, disappointment, even heartache, wishing I could redo some of that early time. Who among us doesn't have twinges of regret for decisions made without knowledge? I'm so thankful that God can uphold me in that remembrance, that I always have access to His compassion, that His grace is sufficient, His love ever present. We do the best we can with the knowledge we have. Knowing some of our decisions in life are more out of self concern than other concern is part of our human-ness. I'm so thankful Jesus is there to support and build us rather than condemning our shortcomings. What a Savior! What abundant grace!

A few weeks later, Carl phoned again to relate another disturbing matter. "Doris called a few weeks ago and asked me to come over and do something with her checkbook. I quickly saw that she hadn't entered a number of checks and also hadn't balanced her bank statement in several months. It was quite a mess," Carl explained with a dry chuckle that sounded more like frustration than humor.

"She can't remember who she's written checks to, so until they come in, we have no way of knowing where they've gone." His exasperation with the situation was palpable. He was sincerely concerned about Mother's affairs and running out of options to help her. It seemed areas of her demise were starting to trip over one another.

"She hasn't clipped her coupon bonds in a number of months either," he continued, "which has left her with a low bank account. However, she has paid her house payment." I was relieved to hear that news until he elaborated. "In fact she paid it three times last month."

I must have audibly groaned. On hearing all this news, I felt confused and baffled. What was happening to Mother's mind? She didn't seem to be thinking clearly, but why? This kind of disorganization, bordering on financial chaos, did not describe the Mother I knew. I began to understand how some elderly people lose their homes even when they have enough money to keep them. They just forget to make payments. In Mother's case, she made too many payments.

About this time, Mother told us Carl had invited her to vacation with him in Europe. (They would be in separate quarters for those of you who are raising an eyebrow!) That's wonderful, I thought. We were so pleased she could fulfill this life long dream. Because of my father's preoccupation with work and early death at 62, they had not traveled much. Mother longed to see the world, especially Ireland where her roots were strong. A journey there had been calling her for years.

With her dream vacation coming up, I was puzzled when she phoned to report that she had lost her airline ticket. It turned out she didn't find it until she returned from the trip. The airline did issue her a new one for a penalty fee. Later, she turned in the old one when it showed up. We supposed this could happen to anyone, so we still weren't overly concerned.

All the symptoms I'm describing came on gradually and over a period of several years, so we didn't connect them until much later. Reading them in a list now, it seems obvious in this day and age as to what was happening. At the time, each incident did seem unusual, but isolated events could be rationalized away to nothing. Add to this, that we lived on the other side of the country and seldom saw each other. I took Mother at her word, as always, convincing myself she was just fine. Perhaps there's a bit of "Pollyanna" in me too. These were just occasional lapses. Everyone has lapses, right?

Some months later when we visited Mother, we had the opportunity to see some of her changes and peculiar behavior up close. First we noticed her glasses frequently disappeared causing what seemed like a continual search to find them. She also hid her car keys and forgot where she put them. Once, Aunt Betty, who lived a couple of blocks away, determined not to leave Mother's home until she found the keys. After much searching, she located them in an obscure drawer in the kitchen. No one had a clue why they were there, including Mother, of course.

When we returned home, we continued to receive calls from Carl. He reported that when Mother did have possession of her keys and drove her car, other curious things happened. Although she had lived in Mesa for seventeen years, she began to occasionally get lost. One or two incidents of this could be brushed off, but the frequency of these episodes increased until it became alarming. Whenever this happened, she called Carl, Aunt Betty, or Dolores, my father's former caretaker who had become a dear friend, to come pick her up. While still on the phone, her friends asked her to look around and try to describe her whereabouts. With a little prodding, they usually figured out her location and proceeded to rescue her.

Several times after calling for help, however, she promptly left the phone booth (this was way before cell phones) and walked home. Somehow she found her way, but then had no idea where she had left the car. Carl would then drive to the location she'd identified and, not finding Mother, he would scout the area and return to her home. Together they would fetch the car. Other times, she left the car and walked home without calling anyone. Interestingly, she always found her way home. Then she and Carl would drive around town until they found the car. Happily, they located it each time. Although these episodes didn't happen frequently, they were beginning to occur enough to indicate cause for concern.

Think about it though...who hasn't occasionally "misplaced" their car at a mall? I have several times. There are occasions when I've come out the wrong door and looked all over the parking lot before realizing what I'd done. One time, my husband, Bill, and I were at a beach on Lake

Michigan. We walked the beach, explored a lighthouse, then walked back to the parking lot where we thought we had parked. We walked all over the lot looking for our car but couldn't find it. Stumped, we were about to look in a further lot when Bill began to laugh as though he suddenly had an epiphany. With a twinkle in his eye he rhetorically asked, "Betsy, where is the car?"

"Ohhhhh," I responded, returning the grin. We had walked to the beach from our campsite. The car was back at the campground.

A Visit

At Christmas time Mother made a trip to Michigan to visit us for the holidays. Meeting her at the airport, I quietly gasped in astonishment as I watched her walk toward us. My heart sank as she approached with the silly smile of a lost, confused child. My normally well kempt, cultured mother looked something akin to a bag lady. Decked in an outdated mink stole, a house dress, and every day walking shoes, her hair was askew and slightly matted and her eyes wore a somewhat demented look. My first response was one of embarrassment, maybe even shame. I wanted to shield her, somehow protect her from the stares of others as they picked up their "normal" looking family and friends. How could Mother go out in public looking like that? What had gotten into her? She just wasn't acting like herself. Yet underneath all the charade of the moment, I sensed something very complex was going on, but I couldn't quite define it. It hadn't been that long since I'd seen her, but she looked as though years had passed, not months.

Agitated and distracted, Mother spent the week pacing around our house. Not sure what to do with herself and with an obvious inability to focus, her face strained as if trying to connect one thought with another, to somehow make sense of this new world she lived in. The week wore on with mounting tension for all of us. Now intolerant of children, she accused our then seven-year-old son, Mike, of outlandish deeds. She was convinced he was rummaging through her suitcase and stealing things. Mike, a sweet and gentle child, was confused and sought out our comfort and understanding.

"Honest, Mommy, I would never touch grandma's things."

"Of course you wouldn't, Mike," I sympathized, drawing him close as his little pained eyes begged us to believe him. "Grandma is not acting normal, and we will just have to be patient." He breathed a sigh of relief as we soothed his anguished sobs. For the rest of the week he hovered close to us for safety, not exactly our dream of a grandmother/grandson relationship.

Near the close of her visit, I soberly told Bill I wasn't sure we could ever have my mother visit in our home again. What a horrible thought! This was the woman who raised me, nurtured me, listened to and cared about me all through my childhood. We had always been close and had a warm, loving relationship. It tore at my heart to think things had deteriorated to the point that I would actually not welcome her in my home.

Little did I know what was coming. We still thought she was just becoming a bit senile. Now, it almost seems I must have been in some sort of denial in those days. Mother's downward spiral just didn't fit my neat little world. Mother's don't change. They're supposed to be there for you forever, aren't they?

It was the late 1980's and Alzheimer's disease was not yet widely recognized. Understanding of Alzheimer's in those days was as veiled to the outsider as it was to the one imprisoned by it.

4
Angel in Disguise

With all this as background, you may understand now why I was flying to Arizona. I had finally understood that something was amiss with Mother and she needed some family attention. This trip to Arizona was the first of several trips. As I sat on the plane, I was in a contemplative mood.

Preparing for this trip, I had tried to deal with my own confusion about Mother's state of mind and had tried to prepare myself through much prayer. In phone conversations I continued to sense Mother's confusion and general disorientation in life. I prayed in earnest, *Lord, please give me an extra measure of mercy and compassion.* I even spent several weeks thinking and focusing on merciful thoughts. I wanted to treat her with patience and understanding in spite of her strange behavior. Remembering the anxiety I had experienced when she had visited us, I knew it would take perseverance and wisdom beyond what I knew I had apart from God.

On the plane, as I met Martha in the seat next to me, I recalled that I had been diligently praying one thing specifically. *Lord, please send someone into my life who can help prepare me for what to expect and how to respond to Mother.* Having no elderly people among my close acquaintances in Michigan, I lacked a seasoned resource person from whom to draw counsel. It looked like it would just be God and me in this one. Yet, I felt lonely and somewhat isolated. I needed God to show Himself strong, to be my refuge, my shield and hiding place in a tangible way. I needed a person who could speak to me with insight, wisdom, and understanding.

I was headed to Arizona with the task of moving Mother into a retirement home, a move that was not exactly her choice. Sorting and packing Mother's belongings would be a daunting task, and knowing her heart was not in it might prove to be overwhelming. Although she lived in a comfortable ranch house with adequate space, like most Americans, she had accumulated a massive amount of things over the years. Since Cynthia lived in New York, we had decided to take turns preparing for the move. The first shift was mine. Cynthia would fly down several weeks later and continue the packing process.

With Mother in an altered state of mind, her ability to communicate about what to pack and what to sell concerned me. Recalling her pacing, agitation, accusations, and lapses in communication from our visit at Christmas, I sensed a measure of anxiety rising in my own soul. We would have a whole house to sort through. As much as I love throwing things away, this home contained Mother's treasures. At the same time, I knew she may not be capable of helping with decisions. I was moving into uncharted water and would be dependent on God to supply all I needed for this trip. Little did I know that God had already gone ahead of me and prepared a sweet lady named Martha on the plane sitting right next to me, ready to meet my need for wisdom.

As I sat back in my airline seat on this first trip, I noticed Martha was about my mother's age. Her pleasant demeanor gave a sense that she was approachable. After all, she had greeted me as she sat down. The soft curls of her short gray hair framed her welcoming countenance as she gave me an inviting smile. The warmth and compassion in her eyes and a smile that seemed to be set on her face eventually beckoned a flow of conversation. She had such an expression of love and openness that I somehow knew she would be a good listener. *Lord, could she be the answer to my prayer?* We began talking, and I soon realized that God had indeed placed this kindhearted lady next to me. She turned out to be an angel in disguise, an answer to my prayer.

Without hesitation, I found myself pouring out my concerns and apprehensions about my mother and her situation. Martha listened attentively. I felt like a dam broke in me, and a river of words and emotion were piling on top of one another. When I finally took a breath, she took my hand and with a sincere look, she calmly spoke to my heart. "I can relate to your situation, Betsy, because I too dealt with a frail and ailing mother many years ago."

I wondered if she was a teacher because she then proceeded to give me five very practical guidelines for dealing with my mother's situation. Her words felt like they were straight from the heart of God, a soothing balm to my soul. I had never met Martha before, yet I was very aware that God had placed her in the seat next to me as a way of answering my heartfelt prayer. Doesn't the Bible say that if we lack wisdom, we can ask for it? And He even promises to give it to us generously (James 1:5). God's wisdom poured from Martha's lips that day as we flew above the puffy white clouds. Her words proved invaluable and equipped me with encouragement and strength for the task at hand.

What she shared became my first five "**Key Principles**" for dealing with a very difficult situation. God was beginning to prepare and equip me through Martha's counsel.

Over the coming months many more principles were added, but these five embedded themselves deeply within my heart and became a cornerstone for all the others. They were so practical and actually proved not hard to implement. At first I had to consciously apply them to situations, but as time went on they became a natural part of my communication and directly affected my interactions with Mother.

Key Principle #1 - Preserve your mother's dignity and integrity at any cost was my new friend's first piece of advice. From that suggestion, I decided that I would try to include Mother in as much of the decision making as her capabilities would allow.

Key Principle #2 – Be sure to initiate affection. I could do this with hugs, holding her hand, rubbing her back, and telling her I love her. Yes, I could easily implement that idea. We had always been affectionate with one another.

Key Principle #3 - Let love be your guide to maintaining peace and unity. I decided to make a commitment not to argue. During the week, this lesson became a valuable tool for wholesome attitudes. I was reminded of the Scripture that says, *"...Do your work heartily as unto the Lord..."* (Col. 3:23). I decided to treat Mother as I would treat the Lord.

Key Principle #4 - Remember victims of senility are not hard of hearing. I tried to be careful what I said in Mother's presence. In her increasing paranoid state, she often thought people were talking about her. This piece of advice would keep me in balance and help me to honor her.

Key Principle #5 – Offer prayer and read Scripture with her. I was about to find that this suggestion would pull all the others together.

5
Rhema

As the plane landed, I sincerely and fervently thanked my new friend. Amidst hugs, she wished me well as we parted ways. Knowing our paths would probably never cross again in this life, I watched as she reunited with her own family. Keenly aware that God had put her in the seat next to me on the plane, I now felt equipped with her words of wisdom. They would prove invaluable for the tasks I would encounter in coming days.

The Bible has two words for "Word." One is "Logos," which is Greek for the entire written Word, i.e. the Bible. The second is "Rhema" and refers to a personal word spoken by God for a specific situation. When Jesus told Peter to walk on water, it was a particular word for him. It wasn't a call for all Christians to walk on water, and there was no intent for a doctrine of walking on water to be fashioned. It was specific direction for Peter alone.

Matthew 4:4 says, *"Man shall not live by bread alone but by every **word** that proceeds out of the mouth of God."*

Word in this verse is translated from rhema. We are to live by every personal word we hear from God.

Again, in Romans 10:17 we read, *"So faith comes from hearing, and hearing by the **word** of Christ."* If we think about it, when have we had leaps of faith? For me, it's often been when the Lord speaks something specific and personal to my heart. Rhema words, of course, must always align themselves with the logos (written word) and often are verses of the Bible. The rhema words Martha spoke to me were clearly personal as to what I needed at that time, and each one lined up perfectly with the heart of God as seen in principles from the Bible. They were principles of loving, gentle precepts that brought peace and understanding. Clearly God had spoken to my heart, and I thanked Him for answered prayer.

This supply from the Lord became the beginning of many answered prayers over the next few years. God showed Himself strong as "Jehovah Jireh," my Provider, at the point of every need throughout my time of caring for Mother. There were occasional tense moments, times of sheer frustration, and a number of incomprehensible situations. Suffering is part of life and even promised in the Bible. With that knowledge, I was comforted knowing God would never leave me nor forsake me. His mercy and compassion surrounded this season of trial, and I met Him in fresh, new ways that further fashioned our relationship into something deeper and more abiding.

As God walked close to me, I learned to trust Him, cling to Him, and rely on Him through all the unusual encounters I met in the ensuing years. My roots grew deep into the rich soil of His character and love as I experienced His provision in every circumstance. He became my hope, my joy, and my peace in the midst of many strange scenarios. He became my strength and my comfort, showing me that no matter what came my way, He would take my hand and supply what I needed in the moment, teaching me along the way to be content and to rest in His abiding love.

Join me now as we travel deeper into the nuances of Mother's Alzheimer's journey.

6
Preparations for the Move

Sorting and separating Mother's things began all too quickly upon my arrival. Remembering Martha's encouragement to preserve Mother's integrity, I sought to engage her in as many decisions as possible regarding what to take to her new apartment and what to send to auction. A project I thought she would enjoy involved organizing her shoes, those to take and those to eliminate. Mother loved shoes and had a closet full for every occasion, though many were outdated. I knew it would be difficult for her to part with any of her shoes, but I envisioned her enjoying the process of creating two neat piles of boxed shoes, those to go and those to stay.

It didn't take long to realize that she needed assistance even with the simplest tasks. Her best effort found her removing all the shoes from their boxes and placing them in one large, confused pile, no two mates together. I had to reason with myself, that though there were boxes and shoes everywhere and the mess worse than when she began, at least she felt part of the process and was having a delightful time. Mother seemed unaware that she was not accomplishing a thing. Just playing with the shoes kept her occupied and content.

Next, I assigned her the job of sorting through her jewelry, again selecting pieces to be sold or given away. Within minutes, I realized this task was also too difficult, but she did spend a wonderful hour playing with the jewelry, looking at each piece and moving it from one pile to another. She reminded me of a three year old child, without a care in the world, involved in a fun project on the simplest level.

Later in the day, as we were folding sheets and boxing them, she excitedly cautioned me, "Don't let the sheets touch the floor, Betsy!" Startled by the force of her command, I raised the sheet up over my head, at the same time wondering why they couldn't touch the floor. I know some people are picky about dirt, but her carpet looked clean to me.

With sheets raised, I asked, "Mother, why don't you want the sheets to touch the floor?"

Her sharp retort caught me off guard. "The carpet is full of bugs, you know! I hear them crunching under my feet with every step!" Her brow curled with the serious intent of her demeanor.

Hmmm, I thought...*I don't see any bugs, nor do I hear any crunching. What is she talking about?* The telltale pesticide odor in the house now seemed to make sense. She had mentioned that she had recently had her whole house exterminated to the tune of $900 to rid the house of bugs. Convinced they were still there, I learned that she sometimes spent whole days vacuuming in an effort to eliminate them. In her imagination, insects were everywhere.

This type of behavior, of course, is a hallucination. Webster's defines hallucinations as *"the apparent perception of sights and sounds that are not actually present."* Only Mother experienced the bugs in the carpet. In reality they did not exist. I later learned that hallucinations are a characteristic sometimes observed in an Alzheimer's victim.

How unnerving it must be for a person to think something is there when it isn't. As Mother's brain function deteriorated, many aberrant thought patterns surfaced. Her fear and repulsion of the bugs was a very real obstacle in her thinking process.

Her fetish for cleanliness spread to other venues as well. At times, she had to be fetched from public restrooms after a fifteen or twenty minute absence. Once, when we went out to dinner, Mother excused herself to go to the restroom. After about twenty minutes, we wondered if there was a problem.

Aunt Betty excused herself from the table and slipped into the restroom. There she found Mother meticulously cleaning the sinks with paper towels.

Her obsession spread to neatness too. When I sorted her clothing, I soon found out why she had trouble finding sweaters she wanted to wear. One morning I noticed that she seemed agitated about getting dressed. "I can't find my blue sweater, Betsy."

Simple logic led to my response, "Well, let's look in your chest of drawers where you keep them." As I opened each drawer, my eyes were met with a cloud of white paper and plastic bags. She had carefully wrapped each sweater in tissue paper and enclosed it in a plastic bag. Layer upon layer of tissue and bags lined each drawer. There was no way to tell which sweater was which without opening the bags and unfolding the tissue paper. When I explained to her why she had so much trouble locating her sweaters, she responded as though it was a new thought. Her mind was unable to connect the idea of the wrapped sweaters with the corresponding idea that she couldn't find her sweaters.

So much of Alzheimer's is loss of connections in or between thoughts. Normal people connect thoughts and ideas so naturally that we don't even think about the process that goes on. In Alzheimer's it becomes difficult to connect the dots, to see how A is related to B.

As she stood by nervously watching, I removed each sweater from its plastic bag, removed the tissue and returned it to the drawer. Mother wasn't sure about this process until I explained that they would stay clean in the drawer without being wrapped.

"Isn't it nice to be able to see your sweaters now?" I asked. She agreed that was a good thing. For now, having forgotten why she wrapped them in the first place, the ability to find her sweaters outweighed her fixation on neatness. Gathering up the mounds of tissue and bags, I quietly disposed of them, hoping she wouldn't become too agitated and want to rewrap the sweaters.

Prayer

With all the work of preparing for the move, I knew I wanted the Lord to be at the center of all our activities and decisions. So, as Martha had suggested praying with Mother, I initiated a time of prayer each morning as we sat down to breakfast. Taking her hands in mine, we bowed our heads and turned our hearts toward God, inviting him into every aspect of our day. Mother seemed so childlike during these times, so innocent and vulnerable. These were sweet times for both of us.

We prayed for our attitudes toward each other and for kindness to be on our lips. The Lord faithfully honored each prayer we sent forth during that visit. For the most part we had a prosperous week filled with love and enjoyment of each other even in the midst of the chaos that was overtaking Mother's mind.

7
Avoiding Quarrels

L ate one afternoon, I was sorting through Mother's storage room, a spacious area lined with shelves adjacent to the kitchen. I felt especially hot that day. The temperature outside was close to 80 degrees and yet Mother, feeling cool, had turned the heat on in the house. I'm quite sure it all gathered in that storage closet. I was dripping in perspiration. After going through box after box, I toyed with the idea of just throwing the rest of them out without inspecting one more carton. I was about to pull down one of the last boxes when Mother appeared with a twinkle in her eye. "You know what's in that box, don't you Betsy?"

"No, I have no idea," I replied, feeling irritated.

"Well, you might want to take a look before you throw it away."

Ok, I'm exhausted, but I'll look in this box to appease you, I thought.

Well... I'll have to say, she got me on that one. The box was extremely heavy as I bumped it off the top shelf and clunked it onto the floor. I gingerly opened the top not knowing what this mystery box might contain. Amazed at my find, I was certainly glad in my worn out state of mind that I hadn't just disposed of it. The box was filled with my father's life long coin collection, one I had forgotten he had.

That evening was spent sorting through a variety of old coins wondering what they might be worth. Feeling rejuvenated by what I had stumbled onto, I covered the living room floor with assorted piles and counted coins late into the night. The next day Mother agreed to accompany me to a local coin shop to find out the value of her treasure. How happy we were when they bought the whole collection and handed us a check for $10,000. We joyfully headed to the bank and deposited it into her account. That had turned into a very pleasant morning.

During the afternoon, however, after a tedious day of sorting and boxing items, Mother accused me of something. I don't even remember what it was. Accusations became more frequent as she felt the stress of the move with all of her belongings in disarray. Hot, drenched, tired, and in need of a shower, I turned to her and curtly stated, "Mother, I think you're a bit confused."

Her sharp retort followed. "You're the confused one, dear!"

At that instant the Lord reminded me of the third piece of advice I had received from my airline angel, "Don't argue; strive for peace and unity." In a split second I regained my composure, made no verbal response, took a deep breath, made a conscious choice and smiled.

"Let's take a break and have a cold drink, Mother, and you can tell me about some of the things we discovered in the storage room."

In this situation and many others, I sensed God's presence and his help in equipping me with a softer response. Had He not prepared me so specifically with just the wisdom I needed in this kind of situation, I'm sure I would have lost my temper more often. God's timing and gentle reminders were perfect.

Later, I was to learn that a common response of Alzheimer's victims is to blame others for things they themselves do wrong. I had read somewhere that one of the parts of the brain that closes down early is the part that tells you that you have a problem, or that you've forgotten or made a mistake. So the natural response is for the person to think that others are the cause of anything that seems amiss. This happened with Mother in a variety of situations in days that followed. For instance, if she couldn't find her keys, her logic was that someone must have taken them. If she

47

misplaced an item of clothing, someone had stolen it. If a family member or a caretaker was in the vicinity, they must be the perpetrators of these injustices. When I mentioned I thought Mother was confused, her reality said that was not true. Therefore, I must be the confused one. It's amazing that when I understood why Mother did some things, compassion had a chance to rise up. No wonder Proverbs exhorts us forty eight times regarding understanding. Proverbs 2:2 sums it up with, *"Make your ear attentive to wisdom, Incline your heart to understanding."*

Mind Set

As we finished the difficult and tiring week of sorting and boxing, I felt God had undertaken and led in every aspect. I experienced rich blessings, watching for and being aware of His hand in each situation. I was reminded of Romans 8:6 which says, we are to walk not according to the flesh, but according to the Spirit. *"For the mind set on the flesh is death, but the mind set on the Spirit is life and peace."*

As I pondered this verse, I noticed the words "mind set" appeared twice. If we make that into one word, "mindset," it could be defined as the direction or outlook of the mind. When we walk in the flesh, our focus is "me," a self-centered approach to relationships and life situations. The outcome of fleshly thinking manifests itself in many negative ways. Things such as anger, lying, depression, lack of forgiveness, fear, anxiety, or being unthankful, all comprise the flesh nature. (Other fleshly qualities can be found in Galatians 5:19-21). When we choose fleshly attitudes, we rob ourselves of participation in the kingdom of God which is described in part in Romans 14:17 as *"...righteousness, peace and joy in the Holy Spirit."* Surely, walking in the Spirit produces life and peace. Interestingly, a simple way to know we are walking in the Spirit is when the fruit of the Spirit is evident in our lives.

Galatians 5:22 lists *"...love, joy, peace, patience, kindness, goodness, faithfulness, gentleness, and self-control"* as the fruit of the Spirit. At any given moment in my days with Mother, I knew I could do a spot check as to whether I was walking in the flesh or in the Spirit. I would know according to the "mindset" I had chosen for the situation at hand. Realizing it was a choice helped me through the trials I faced in preparing for her move.

Key Principle #6 - Spot check your mindset. In addition to Martha's five strategic principles given to me on the plane, the Lord gave me twenty more which I will share throughout my story. Key Principle #6, checking my mindset, became an invaluable tool for keeping my thought life healthy. When things were out of kilter, I knew the solution lay in the examination of my thoughts and the attitudes they fostered. Adjustments were sometimes in order. I was reminded that attitudes in life are a choice. It's easy to set our mind on blaming others for attitudes and responses that we have chosen. Defending ourselves, we accuse others of triggering certain responses in us. When other people behave in a certain way, our tendency can be to justify inappropriate responses that are really our own heated or simply "bad reactions." No one "makes us" behave badly. We choose that ourselves. That can be tough to acknowledge.

In reality, we are each responsible for the attitudes we choose. I remember a time when our girls, Kim and Laurie, were young and I had a problem with irritability. Without realizing it, I had given myself permission to be short-tempered over many things. It was a pattern in my life until one day Bill, in his loving way said, "You know, Betsy, you don't have to be irritable. It's a choice." With those words, my first reaction was to be upset with him, but upon considering what he said, I realized he was right. Irritability was a choice. Although I had no control over how others might act toward me, or what they might say to me, I did have control over my responses.

Calling on the Holy Spirit to begin operating His self-control in my life, I made a decision that day. Realizing I was the one who set the atmosphere in our home, I felt convicted to choose better attitudes and to put aside moodiness. That meant that instead of choosing irritability, I would take personal responsibility for my own reactions or responses to life. What, at first, had felt like a rebuke from Bill, ended up loosing in me a refreshing freedom. I realized I had options in my behavior. I did not have to be a slave to my feelings. I was reminded of Galatians 5:1. *"It was for freedom that Christ set us free; therefore keep standing firm and do not be subject again to a yoke of slavery."* There is a freedom that comes when we are no longer enslaved by poor choices.

I think this concept was further sealed in my thinking when I helped out with the 2000 Census. My job was to visit homes where the Census either wasn't received or wasn't sent in. Throughout this time, I visited about 175 homes in our area. An interesting observation began to unfold about the second week and continued for the duration of the month. As I visited different homes, I met all kinds of people from all walks of life. While most people were cordial, treating me with kindness and respect, I observed some were very angry and full of contempt. At the same time, I also noticed that people's moods and reactions to my presence really had nothing to do with me. I realized I was not responsible for how they greeted me or treated me in the interview. I was only responsible for my behavior towards them, which I chose to be gracious, kind, calm, and polite.

Although I maintained consistency throughout the census, at some houses my kindness was met with irritation and even defiance. It was so obvious in this niche time when I met lots of people that their behavior was their own choice. Each one acted out of who they were, just as I acted out of who I was. It was so enlightening and helpful to observe this day after day. While my mood was consistent, their responses varied.

I share this because it is so easy and common to assume that if someone is upset with us, then we must have done something wrong. That is not necessarily true. It's also freeing to know that others are responsible for their behavior and reactions. We are not responsible for the behavior of other people. It's easy for people to "feel" responsible for someone else's distress. But remember, we have a choice in our own response to people regardless of whether they treat us with thoughtfulness or disgust. We are accountable for our behavior, and they are responsible for their reply.

It was interesting to note that several times a person who initially greeted me with an irritated mood, upon seeing my consistent behavior, calmed down and also behaved in a friendly manner. Fortunately, no one swore at me. I am reminded of Proverbs 15:1, *"A gentle answer turns away wrath...."*

Just as I again observed the value of consistent responses in my census experience, with Mother I learned the importance of choosing quiet, calm attitudes and words. I wanted my behavior to be what she needed, not just a selfish reaction.

8
Time Disorientation

About midnight one night, still awake, I laid in bed reading. Mother's room was right across the hall from mine, and she had gone to bed about 8:30 P.M. I was surprised to hear her bedroom door open at this late hour and then a few moments later, the front door open. I sat up in bed and pondered what she might be doing. I didn't have a clue. Listening intently, I waited a minute and then all was quiet. Wondering what she could be up to, I slipped out of bed, put on my robe and slippers, and tiptoed cautiously to the front door. Finding it ajar, I peered out into the darkness. All was silent. *Surely Mother wasn't outside*, I thought. *Why would she be out there at midnight?* I hesitated a moment and then quietly whispered, "Mother?"

"Yes," she answered.

Surprised to hear her voice outside, I prompted, "What are you doing out there?"

"I'm looking for the morning paper," she replied in a matter of fact tone.

"Well, it won't be here for hours! It's midnight. Come on in and let's get you back to bed." Reentering the house, I noticed she was fully dressed and had even made her bed. I helped her back into her nightgown, pulled down the covers and tucked her in for the night. This time she remained in her room. I knew she probably wouldn't even recall the incident in the morning.

Disorientation to time became a common and disturbing pattern in Mother's life. I felt troubled and somewhat perplexed as she displayed confusion regarding time. Sometimes, she would get up at three o'clock in the morning and think it was time for breakfast.

One morning, she anxiously awakened me at six o'clock. "Betsy, get up!" Her tone was authoritative yet disturbed.

Sleepily I rolled over, pulled my arm out from the warm covers and tried to focus on my watch. "Why do I need to get up so early, Mother?" I groggily replied.

"Because the workman will be arriving soon," she responded with agitation.

"What time is he coming?" I yawned making my way to the bathroom to wash my face.

"He'll be here at nine o'clock, so you need to hurry."

I checked my watch again. Six o'clock. Something was amiss. Realizing that we had three hours before the workman would arrive, I stopped in my tracks, did an about face and crawled back in bed. Unable to sleep and wondering if Mother was confused, I decided to call the repairman at eight o'clock.

"No, I'm not scheduled to come to your mother's home today," he puzzled. "I'm coming tomorrow, but the appointment is in the afternoon."

If Mother had a doctor appointment, she would be ready to go hours before it was time to leave, pacing the floor, back and forth, back and forth, asking the time every few minutes, sure she would be late. Sometimes I took her early, and we sat in the doctor's office an hour or so before the appointment so that she would be at peace. At times, her anxiety level became so intense that she developed shortness of breath and dizziness. The ability to relax had escaped her. I felt a deep chasm developing between her reality and mine.

In retrospect, my heart went out to her. It must be terrifying to lose your mind. There must be a sort of grasping to find reality and make sense of life. Losing the concept of time must be equally confusing. Events and situations piled up on top of each other, each one demanding immediate attention. Confusion reigned, making sense was no longer an option. There was so much uncertainty in the disorder that now defined her life. The ability to reason, to think clearly, to sort out logically, many of the things that make us human were stolen from my mother, never to be returned.

Lost Keys

Another oddity that I observed involved Mother's compulsion to hoard and hide things. I must have found a dozen jars, coin purses, and cups filled with coins. She had collected quite a stash. I never knew where they would show up. Many of the kitchen drawers I opened had an accumulation of hidden coins tucked in the back.

Stockpiling had become a kind of obsession. Besides hidden coins, almost every day we had to search for her purse, her keys or her glasses. She became so adept at hiding things that sometimes the item wasn't found for days. Her car keys were a case in point. She had hidden them so well that a locksmith was called on to make a new set. When Carl learned that the whole dashboard would have to be removed, he decided they would search further in the house for the keys. After Mother finally located them, she excitedly called Carl, but by the time he arrived she had hidden them again and forgotten why Carl had come over. Recovery was made in time and wisely, Carl removed one set to his house for safe keeping.

Driving Disorientation

The day finally arrived when we felt it was necessary for Mother to give up driving. On her final "lost" episode, she phoned Carl and delivered the words he had grown to dread. "I don't know where I am, Carl."

With what was becoming his routine reply, he asked, "Can you see any street signs or buildings you recognize, Doris?" One last time, Carl patiently awaited her description of her whereabouts. Breathing a sigh of relief, he recognized her location and was able to drive there to pick her up.

Besides getting lost more often, there was also a growing deficit in her coordination and attention span. Clearly, her driving skills were waning. At one point her attention veered from driving and she rear-ended a police car! That kind of thing can have its own repercussions. We won't even go there.

On several occasions, I drove with her as a passenger and somehow survived, but be assured, it was with white knuckles. I was seeing first hand what Carl had tried to explain to me in various phone conversations. Her perception had declined, and she seemed oblivious to other cars, sometimes tailgating and at other times pulling out in front of cars at inappropriate times.

The last time I rode with her as a passenger, she seemed unaware of the traffic around her. After looking both ways, she pulled out onto the highway right in front of a startled driver. As she proceeded to change lanes without looking, I wondered if we would make it home alive. Finally, as she barely put on the brakes in time at a stop light, I realized we could not continue this way. With all the authority I could muster, I sternly dictated a no nonsense directive, "Mother, pull off the road. I'm going to drive."

With mounting anxiety, I recognized both of our lives were in danger if she continued in the driver's seat. Arizona roads are crowded, and decisions must be made rapidly. I was thankful Mother submitted to my dictate without any resistance. Without further hesitation, I dogmatically stated that while I was visiting, I would do the driving. Case closed.

Later that day, after discussing our outing with Bill and Carl, we all felt the time had come that Mother should no longer drive at all. That afternoon I kept her keys when we arrived home. She thought she had lost them again. Though a difficult decision for her to accept, I knew this was the way it had to be. She had already plowed into a police vehicle, and she had frightened me and a number of other drivers in the short time we had driven together. Who knows how many other close calls she had encountered in recent months? It was by God's grace that she hadn't done any serious damage to herself or someone else. In good conscience I knew that to leave her on the road in her present condition would be irresponsible. Ignoring serious potential dangers could have ended tragically for her and possibly for others. Even so, the gradual stripping of her former lifestyle was difficult to watch.

Mother verbalized her objection to my decision that she not drive anymore and had difficulty understanding my reasoning. So much of her independence remained wrapped up in the fact that she could transport herself wherever she wanted to go. She knew she would now be dependent on others to take her to the dentist, the doctor, the store, and any other outings. She hated giving up driving and fought for her rights. Although I felt some guilt in asserting myself in this area of her life, in a way it was a healthy sign that she still had some fight in her. Though many of her abilities were diminishing, she was not defeated by Alzheimer's yet. She still spoke up for some things.

For several days, she mumbled about her car but finally accepted that she couldn't drive without keys. It seemed like a comfortable way for her to transition out of driving, but still, it made me sad to have to deny her the use of her car. One more thing had been stolen from her fleeting life.

Several weeks later Carl put an ad in the paper and sold the car. Thankfully, Mother never noticed or questioned it again.

I'm not sure whether Mother was ever fully aware of the changes taking place in her mind. There seemed to be either a great aptitude for denial or a merciful lack of awareness. Except for one brief moment later in her demise, Mother never acknowledged that anything was wrong with her throughout the years of her eccentric behavior.

9
Tests

In spite of all the unusual behavior we were witnessing, we still didn't know for sure if Mother had Alzheimer's disease. At this time Carl made arrangements for her to undergo a brain scan and an EEG to determine the cause of her memory loss. Having another close friend with Alzheimer's, Mother's symptoms concerned him greatly. He wanted to know if Alzheimer's could be identified in her brain or if her symptoms were associated more with senility, or possibly with side effects from her medications. We all wanted to know what we were dealing with. Mother resisted the idea of tests concerning her failing memory but reluctantly agreed to visit the doctor to take them. Unfortunately, the doctor was not able to conclusively say yet if it was Alzheimer's. However, he determined that her brain was shrinking, and there were shadows indicating dead brain cells, a typical sign of the disease.

Unfortunately, Alzheimer's cannot be decisively diagnosed without an autopsy after death, but in later stages symptoms can be quite convincing. Occasionally, dementia patients are diagnosed with Alzheimer's disease but may be victims of a number of other ailments. In later stages of Alzheimer's, after the observation of a number of classic symptoms, a fairly reliable diagnosis can be given. I appreciated the doctor's explanation for what it was worth, but we were still left with very little understanding of what was coming.

Following the tests, Mother recalled the ordeal with hurt and denial. She became defensive and often told us she was not crazy and how offended she was with the tests. To her, being pushed to endure this kind of examination was demeaning. Her interpretation was that her dignity was in question.

"Carl thinks I'm crazy and I'm not," she repeated over and over. "He hurt me deeply by putting me through those tests." My heart stung hearing those words. This was my beloved mother and Carl's dear friend. We would never purposely do anything to injure her emotionally. In no way did we have any thought of dishonoring her integrity. It was our goal to esteem her but at the same time care for her as we observed a curious chain of events. It was painful to watch her imagination make assumptions and cast negative interpretations on the help we were seeking for her benefit.

In retrospect, there are things I would probably have done differently. This was one of them. It would have been better if I had simply told her she needed a checkup. I'm certain she would have agreed to that without feeling threatened. The doctor could have done the tests and reported results to us. I doubt if Mother would have inquired about the results, nor would she have understood them if she had.

Mother was caught in such a helpless illness, a disease that has been likened to a thunderstorm in the brain, one which destroys the brain's nerve cells and synapses, the connectors that help cells to communicate with one another. There was no cure in 1991 when Mother's Alzheimer's became full blown. Even now, many years later, there is still no cure. The medical community does offer medications now which help to allay symptoms, and there are natural products which claim to help, but ultimately, they don't stop the progression of the disease. Those close to a victim must simply accept the disease and hopefully rely on God, family, and friends for comfort and support. Thankfully, I also found a support group later in her illness. It was sad to watch the deterioration of my beautiful mother, remembering how alive, active, and independent she had once been, knowing it would never be that way again in this life.

Statistics

It's been over twenty years since Mother had Alzheimer's. There were 4 million Americans suffering from Alzheimer's in 1991. In 2012 the Alzheimer's Association reports there are 5.4 million. By 2050, it is expected that number will rise to 16 million and that's just in America. The number of unpaid caregivers for people with this disease is 15 million.

While deaths from other illnesses such as stroke, breast cancer, heart disease, and HIV have decreased in the past eight years, deaths from Alzheimer's and dementia have increased by a staggering 66%. Whereas many other ailments can be either prevented or cured, Alzheimer's cannot. It is the 6th leading cause of death in America. Almost everyone knows of someone with Alzheimer's today.[1]

10
Reflection

I was so thankful Mother had received Jesus as her personal Lord and Savior earlier in life. Although there was no hope to prevent or cure Alzheimer's, there is always hope in God. Living with eternal values made all the difference as we walked along the crooked road before us. I experienced a certain peace knowing that Mother was in God's hands and that when she would eventually meet the Lord face to face, He would restore her to perfect health. The promises of Scripture sustained us both during this trial. With that knowledge, I could look at this disease as just a temporary ailment, even though I didn't really know my mother for the last three years of her life. She had completely changed, but in retrospect, those years were so momentary compared to eternity.

Through all the hard times, I knew in the secret places of my heart, that on the other side I would have my mother back as a whole person to enjoy for all eternity. This is the wonderful everlasting hope shared by Christians. It's a sure hope that offers much peace and the ability to endure life's struggles. Hebrews 11:1 explains hope as connected with faith. *"Now faith is the assurance of things hoped for, the conviction of things not seen."* Even though I could not see details of the future, by faith I had a firm assurance that in the end God would have something good waiting.

I was thankful for Scripture that spoke directly to this situation. II Corinthians 5 has several verses appropriate to anyone walking through a difficult time. Verses 1 and 2 speak of our mortal body as a tent or a house when it says, *"For we know that if the earthly tent which is our house is torn down, we have a building from God, a house not made with hands, eternal in the heavens. For indeed in this house we groan, longing to be clothed with our dwelling from heaven."*

Going on, in verses 5-7, we read, *"Now He who prepared us for this very purpose is God, who gave to us the Spirit as a pledge. Therefore, being always of good courage, and knowing that while we are at home in the body we are absent from the Lord for we walk by faith, not by sight."*

I believe that behind all the things that we see, the things that seem to be the reality that we walk in as we go through life, there is a greater reality in the plan of God which is not seen but encountered in the spirit by faith. If I had not believed that God was ultimately in control and could be trusted even in the unknown of this disease, I would have despaired. If I had not believed that everything that came into my life was first sifted through the hands of God, I would have been distraught. My sentiments matched David's from Psalm 27:13 when he said, *"I would have despaired unless I had believed that I would see the goodness of the Lord in the land of the living."* I had hope. God's word sustained me even on the darkest days.

I received an email, one of those anonymous emails that contained a lesson. It seems appropriate to include it here. It was called "Eagles in a Storm." Did you know that an eagle knows when a storm is approaching long before it breaks? The eagle will fly to some high spot and wait for the winds to come. When the storm hits, he sets his wings so that the wind picks him up, lifting him above the storm. Then while the storm rages below, the eagle soars above it. The eagle does not escape the storm. He simply uses the storm to lift him higher. He rises on the winds that bring the storm.

When the storms of life come upon us, and all of us will experience them, we can rise above them by setting our minds and our belief toward God. Storms do not have to overcome us. We can allow God's power to lift us above them. God enables us to ride the wind of the storms that bring sickness, tragedy, failure, and disappointment into our lives. We can soar beyond the storm. Remember, it is not the burdens of life that weigh us down; it is how we handle them, how we respond to them. The Bible says, *"Those who hope in the Lord will renew their strength. They will soar on wings like eagles..."* (Isa. 40:31). (NIV)

Key Principle #7 - Realize that God is in control and can be trusted even in the unknown. When things seemed out of control by sight, I reminded myself that God was still on the throne and that He still had a perfect plan in all things. He was not unaware of the situations I encountered with Mother. He had not lost sight of our need for help. He was not surprised by what was happening. He saw and He cared.

A lesson taught in Genesis 16:11-13 involves Hagar and her son Ishmael. Hagar was distraught as she found herself in a literal "wilderness" experience. The angel of the Lord appeared to her with words of encouragement that she was to name her son Ishmael, which means "God hears." The angel told her that God had "...given heed to her affliction." Hagar then said, "...You are a God who sees...."

In my experience with my mother in the wilderness of Alzheimer's, I felt I personally met with the God who sees, hears, and gives heed. He was securely on His throne and proved Himself faithful over and over again.

He wanted me to walk by faith and not by sight. I was in His training camp to learn this principle at a deeper level. In

Romans 8:28 He promised that I could *". . . know that God causes all things to work together for good to those who love God, to those who are called according to His purpose."* I knew that I loved God, and I knew He had called me to be His own. Therefore, it followed that whatever happened in my life, He was in control and could be trusted. I derived great comfort as I clung to that knowledge. My faith grew as I contemplated His concern for our situation.

Psalm 25:10 states, *"All the paths of the Lord are loving kindness and truth to those who keep His covenant and His testimonies."* I concluded that even though, by sight, the trial Mother and I were going through was difficult, it was a path on which we ran headlong into the loving kindness of the Lord time after time.

This particular ailment was an opportunity for growth and character development in my life. My prayer was that I wouldn't miss a single lesson the Lord wanted to teach me through the many responsibilities I had with my mother.

11
Finishing Tasks

My week in Arizona quickly drew to an end. I had done the first pruning of Mother's belongings, sorting things to be taken to the retirement home and things to be auctioned. I don't think Mother ever fully realized that all of her belongings were not going to accompany her to her new location. I saw no reason to tell her. It would only cause confusion. She was perplexed enough when the auctioneer came to look over what we would be selling. I tried to shield her from hearing our conversation, but her ears were pretty sharp, and again her anxiety level went up.

I had filled boxes as discreetly as possible, but she still insisted on taking all fifty plus handkerchiefs and thirty some belts that for years had not gone with any outfit. I've heard that elderly people often cling to their worldly possessions as if their personal identity were somehow dependent on a handkerchief or a belt. With so many of her personal belongings being removed from her life, I could understand how familiar things had become increasingly more valued. Change is usually hard for most people, and Mother's life was being turned upside down. Being surrounded with familiar things brought a sense of comfort. She would be going to all new surroundings and many of her things would not be accompanying her in the move. Yet, when it was all said and done, she never appeared to miss anything that was left behind.

Before the move, I had taken Mother to a lawyer with the purpose of acquiring papers for Power of Attorney, as I would now be taking responsibility for her finances. Not knowing much about legal matters, I retained a simple Power of Attorney. In retrospect, I should have gotten a Durable Power of Attorney for health issues as well as finances. Live and learn! I did get that later, but when I did, Mother was beyond being able to write and had to sign with an X. Fortunately, her X was never brought into question regarding any official issues.

Now it was my sister, Cynthia's, task to fly to Arizona and actually move Mother and her remaining belongings. At that time, Cynthia, my vivacious, beautiful, energetic, blue eyed, blond sister, lived in New York City and was an opera singer. Her colorful career, perfectly suited to her musical gifts, required that she travel frequently throughout the United States and, in fact, all over the world. She had sung before kings and princes and performed on stage with such notables as Pavarotti, Jerome Hines, and Joan Sutherland. You can tell I was very proud of her, as was Mother.

Mother, in her finer years, had traveled with Cynthia to a number of her opera performances. She relished being back stage before a performance, watching Cynthia's makeup artist prep her for her role that evening and the hair stylist, as she adjusted the perfect wig. As Cynthia was assisted in dressing in an ornate gown, Mother wondered at the extraordinary weight of each costume, some as high as fifty pounds. She loved the drama of operas, the opportunity to see her daughter on stage, and the fun of astonishing her seatmates with the knowledge that it was her daughter up there singing. We were all impressed with Cynthia's career. But for this season, Mother became Cynthia's priority.

The retirement home Mother had chosen was located just a few miles from the house she had called home for so many years. She and Carl were familiar with this particular residence in their community, and he felt it would meet Mother's needs very well. Tastefully decorated in shades of mauve and teal, this new location was modern, exquisite, and carefully arranged. The soft colors gave a delightful ambiance, and the cheerful faces of the staff helped us know this would be a friendly environment for Mother's transition. On the entry level, a large sitting room and a beautiful dining room added to its aesthetic grace. It was a classy place, just like my mother.

As we walked into Mother's third floor apartment, there was a bathroom to the right with a wall to wall mirror. Across the hall was a cozy bedroom with space for two beds and her dresser. To the left of the entry was a small kitchenette, and beyond that was a modest, but comfortable living room, always bright with a large sliding glass door leading to a balcony deck. Her balcony overlooked a courtyard boasting a winding creek, an arched walking bridge, and attractive land-scaping. Everything was well-designed and distinguished.

Her meals would be taken in the lovely downstairs dining room where she would be seated with several other elderly residents. It seemed like an ideal location for Mother, well kept, efficient, and with an opportunity for socialization.

With relieved minds, we realized Mother would now be served meals regularly and would, hopefully, gain back the weight she had lost in recent months. Apart from that, her daily living would be fairly independent. Carl would continue to call or look in on her every day. Cynthia and I felt confident that Mother would get along well in this new location.

12
Laundry Dilemma

S everal months after my initial visit to pack for the move, I made another trip to visit Mother. Cynthia joined me this time as we purposed to see how Mother was adjusting to her new environment. We found her doing quite well physically. No longer having to cook her own meals, the dining room served her well, and she had gained back some of her weight.

Though doing better physically, we sadly noted continued mental deterioration. It showed up in many ways. One of the most revealing incidents involved her laundry. She was not yet in the assisted living section of the retirement home, so she was expected to do her own laundry. To my dismay, I discovered a large pile of clothes in her laundry basket and wondered what was going on. Upon questioning her, I pieced together that she hadn't washed any clothes in the three months she had lived in the retirement home. Upon inquiring further, she told me she didn't understand how to run the washer and dryer. Puzzled, I gathered up the

75

mound of unwashed clothing and took Mother into the laundry room, thinking it must be that the appliances were new to her and she just needed some basic help with instructions. Appeased with that thought, I reminded myself that Mother wasn't the mechanical type, so this lapse would make sense.

I pushed open the laundry room door, plopped her basket on the floor and stood with her in front of a fresh white washing machine. Reviewing the instructions, I explained the simple procedure. "Push in the knob, turn to desired washing cycle, and pull the knob out." Mother stood motionless.

I'm not mechanical either and even have a mental block toward learning new mechanical things, but this one seemed uncomplicated, even to me. What could Mother's problem possibly be? She had done laundry for years and these machines were about as basic as they come. It baffled me that she couldn't figure it out. They were not complex machines. I was sure she must be putting me on. That's it, I decided, rolling my eyes. She just wants some attention!

Gently, but with emphasis, I explained again how to run the washer. When she still couldn't do it herself, I clarified the simple process once again and then again. "Push knob in, turn to desired cycle, pull knob out," I repeated with as much patience as I could muster. Noticing a distant, vacant look in her eyes, I suggested we talk through the steps. With agitation, she paused to study the machine. Concentrating with all her effort, I could tell she was trying to focus.

"Push knob in," she slowly began. "Then...then...."
She began to shake her head. Her hands tensed, her face contorted with anxiety, and she began step from side to side. With an anguished cry, she sputtered, "I don't know what comes next, Betsy!"

By then I could tell she was truly trying to concentrate. Her troubled brown eyes darted back and forth across the washer knobs. She began to pace. Her breathing became irregular, and I realized she was hyper-ventilating. In anxious despair, she blurted again, "I don't know what comes next!"

Like a brick, it hit me that my mother sincerely had no idea how to run a washer or dryer. Not only that, but she seemed incapable of learning how to do it. That was as far as she could go. I was astounded. How could this be true? The whole incident seemed surreal to me. How could a person not be able to figure out how to run a washing machine? My mind refused to accept the reality I was observing. With one more unsuccessful attempt, I finally printed out some simple directions and gave them to her in hopes that at a later time she would be more rational. But when "later" came, I discovered she had hidden the directions! They were nowhere to be found. Shaking my head, I realized that Mother would need someone to do her laundry from now on. I would have to look into that before I left. Meanwhile, I started the wash cycle.

Uneducated Guesses

Cynthia and I spent hours discussing Mother's condition. Neither of us knew anything about Alzheimer's disease. We thought Mother was just getting old. Some of our conversations were clearly unenlightened. "It seems like Mother is really having trouble with even the simplest tasks," I would start.

"You know, Betsy, I'm sure much of this is just an act. Mother has always had a lot of actress in her. She loves to embellish and emote," Cynthia would reply.

"Oh, I don't know, Cynthia, she really seems disturbed about doing many things that used to be commonplace to her."

We would eventually get to our next conversation. Cynthia would start, "We've tried for years to get Mother interested in outside activities. I've encouraged her to get involved in an opera guild, and you've tried your best to get her into some of her church's activities. I'm sure if she had occupied herself with more outside activities with adequate mental stimulation, this wouldn't be happening to her now. She just hasn't had enough to occupy her mind over the years."

"Well, I suppose that's a possibility," I replied, "but Mother has never been a club type person. She's content with her parties."

Somehow Cynthia and I, because of lack of knowledge, thought for a time that a deficiency of mental stimulation had somehow left Mother in the predicament she now found herself. We were truly baffled by the obvious mental changes we were observing, not realizing Mother's mind was now sequestered in the dark recesses of Alzheimer's disease. Since then, we have found that it's common for family members to fail to comprehend what's involved in the memory loss of Alzheimer's. And to tell the truth, it is hard to understand and believe that a formerly capable person is no longer able to complete even simple tasks. It was not until later that we grasped that Mother's plight in life had nothing to do with being in clubs or not, reading or not, or her choices regarding any kind of mental stimulation. The break down of her brain was much more complex than any of that.

Up All Night

While Cynthia and I visited Mother, we had decided I would stay with Mother in her apartment, and Cynthia would stay nearby at Aunt Betty's home. The first night was quite an experience for me as I was introduced to Mother's interesting "night life." Around eight thirty, Mother retired to bed while I remained up to read the newspaper. Since Mother had a one bedroom apartment now, I planned to sleep in the extra bed in her room. It seemed like a comfortable and workable situation.

Around ten o'clock, I came to bed, and we soon turned off the light. I pulled the covers up around my neck, closed my eyes and felt myself relax into welcome sleep, but not for long. Within an hour, I was jarred awake when Mother turned on the overhead light and began to pace in and out of the room. In and out, in and out. *What in the world was she doing?*

"Mother, could we turn off the light now and get some sleep?" I drowsily pleaded.

"Ok," she cheerfully agreed. So once more we settled in. The quiet darkness was again a welcome relief to my weary body. Just as I began to drift off for a second time, on went the light, and the pacing resumed. *Oh, no,* I sighed under my breath. *What now?*

Within the next hour Mother was up several times, turning on the light, fidgeting, and pacing. Finally, realizing that sleeping in the same room was not going to work, in desperation for some rest, I opted to move to the living room couch where I spent the rest of the week. Mother, who had always been a considerate person, had lost all concept of thoughtfulness toward others. I don't think she had any idea that she was disturbing my sleep. I couldn't be angry with her because I realized she was not aware she was doing anything annoying. Night life and pacing were just part of the new reality she lived in. I chalked it up to one more odd behavior pattern, one among, what were now becoming, many.

Cleaning Surprises

After getting some much needed sleep on the couch, next on the agenda, I decided to clean out her refrigerator. She had only lived in the retirement home for a few months, but the refrigerator was completely crammed with food. It was hard to find anything because every inch was bulging with edibles, and I was soon to discover, some "not so edibles." Upon checking further into the depths of the refrigerator, I noticed some curious matter that must have been food at one time: curdled milk, hardened crusty bread, and various unidentifiable moldy items. Mother had always been a meticulous housekeeper with a neat and tidy kitchen. Since the retirement home served her meals in a dining room, she really had no need for a refrigerator, but she somehow kept it fully stocked and never threw anything away...ever.

Growing up, I had observed that Mother was a thrifty person when it came to food. She attributed that to having come through World War II and the food lines. So I was used to her saving all leftovers after a meal. Her common routine was to save food until it was no longer usable. In her altered mental state now, she tended to save things way beyond that point. On the positive side, there was lots of room in the refrigerator when I was finished cleaning.

13
Hallucinations and Delusions

Mother remained in this apartment for about six months. During this time we noticed an increase in hallucinations and delusions. She began to collect magazine and brochure covers that had pictures of people on them. Pictures of actors and other celebrities were scattered around her apartment. These people became real in her mind to the point that she developed personal relationships with them and carried on conversations.

One in particular that caused a major fixation was Gunther, the Las Vegas lion tamer. Conversations with him provided many hours of entertainment for Mother. At the mention of his name, her fondness toward him brought a sparkle to her eyes.

"There's a tiger living in my room," she announced one afternoon.

"Oh, there is?" I mused.

"Yes, he stays on my bed. He's quite tame."

My obvious question, "Does it frighten you to have a tiger in your room?"

"Oh, no," she quipped. "Gunther is here with him all the time." "Actually, it's quite nice. I enjoy having them here," she smiled with contentment.

Before long she reported that there were many animals living with her.

"Do you see the animal behind the television?" she asked.

"No, I don't Mother. What do you think it is?" She wasn't sure, but after describing it, I said, "That sounds like an iguana."

"Yes, that's what it is," she said, breathing a sigh of relief to have a name for it.

Key Principle #8 - Accept odd behavior and humor her. I have observed caretakers who become quite flustered and annoyed trying to change some of the eccentric behavior displayed by Alzheimer's victims. This usually meets with resistance. To Mother, her behavior was perfectly normal. While some of her conduct could be redirected into more acceptable channels, much of it had to be accepted for what it was. Fighting it would have caused frustration for both of us. Changing my expectations was the key to accepting her behavior.

It was important for me to continually remind myself that Mother's reality was no longer my reality. We literally lived in two different worlds. Her world was as real to her as mine was to me. To challenge any aspect of her behavior was considered rude and offensive, a violation of her new world view. She truly had no understanding why anyone would object to her actions or words. At best, she seemed confused by my conduct, why I didn't see things her way.

While some erratic behavior could be redirected, I found that in most cases, I had to change my response. In the case of her night wandering, the only solution was for me to move out of the bedroom. Mother could not be responsible for what appeared to be inconsiderate behavior. If I had chosen to dwell on her seemingly thoughtless actions, I would only have made myself miserable. She, on the other hand, would have been oblivious and probably disturbed by my negative posture. With protocol for normalcy abandoned, she would have had no understanding as to why my attitude was unpleasant. For the sake of her comfort, we were both better off by my choice to adhere to the principle of accepting her new behavior as normal for her. Her thinking was marginalized. This was not my mother; this was simply my new mother, with Alzheimer's.

Often, when people act in aberrant ways, there is under-lying motive or intent. This was not the case with Mother. She was not scheming and purposely thinking of things to challenge or upset me. There was no hidden agenda or motive in her behavior, nor was she intentionally trying to be thoughtless. Understanding this proved invaluable in many situations during her demise.

Closely akin to accepting odd behavior by changing my expectations was the principle of humoring Mother. As she related her bazaar stories, I decided to humor her by going along with what she said, regardless of how "off the wall" it sounded. If I chose not to, she became quite troubled and irritated. To her, the animals in her apartment were real. To question her about them would have been an insult although I have to admit a trace of a smile sometimes played on my lips as I pondered how ludicrous and irrational some of her conduct seemed. I found harmony was best maintained by going along with the absurdities, and it seemed to ignite a measure of hope in her.

Gunther became such a real part of her life that she told perfect strangers about him and the entourage of animals living with her. It was interesting, and sometimes embarrassing, for me to watch their reactions. I wanted to protect Mother, but how? In these situations, I tried to catch the eye of the stranger and quietly nod to help them to know I understood they were uncomfortable. Sometimes, when Mother wasn't looking, I would mouth, *"She has Alzheimer's."* They would then give me a knowing nod, or if they weren't familiar with this disease, they would just look puzzled or perplexed, which often described my feelings as well.

Grace is a wonderful gift. I was learning to extend it to Mother in many awkward situations. Admittedly though, at times I was caught off guard and unsure how to respond to her eccentric behavior in public.

Home in her apartment, I would sometimes pause outside her room and observe Mother sitting on her bed with a number of pictures lined up next to her. Animated whispers of conversation wafted from the room as she passed the time in her own little world. It was an odd feeling, knowing that if I said anything, I would be interrupting an intimate conversation. I almost felt like I was violating her privacy by watching at all.

It is interesting that we sometimes look at the elderly as just passing time, and we wonder how hard it must be for them. But looking back, I think time passes differently for people as they get older, especially if they are suffering from dementia.

Mother's focus on pictures took many interesting turns. One evening, she took a picture of a man from a magazine to dinner and placed it on the seat next to hers.

"Why aren't you eating your dinner?" Mother's table companion asked.

"Oh, I don't want to eat until he's been served," she seriously announced, glancing at the picture on the chair next to her. When another lady started to sit down in that chair, Mother showed alarm. With irritation, she asked her to please sit elsewhere. Mother was incensed by the disrespect shown to her picture guest.

Once, after visiting the dentist, she took home a brochure with the dentist's picture on the cover. She later told me the dentist had moved in with her. Then she proceeded to phone his office and make "him" an appointment. Fortunately the office caught on to what was happening and were not surprised when I called to explain. I'm still trying to figure out how a dentist could have an appointment with himself. This incident was one more pointer to the breach in Mother's brain.

Looking at pictures of my family and of my father disturbed Mother as well. With pursed lips, she huffed in an intolerant tone, "There's a man in my bedroom and he keeps watching me." I determined it was my father's picture, and shortly after, I noticed she had turned it down on her dresser.

I could only guess that she no longer recognized him. He was now an outsider, an intruder.

Since pictures of my family were on the television, she explained to me how disgusting it was that we all lived with her now. "They can afford a place of their own. I don't see why they have to live in my apartment. It makes it so crowded in here," she curtly lamented. On one hand, she realized I was her daughter whom she loved, but on the other hand, her daughter was that "unwelcome visitor" in the picture. Clearly, her brain was not making connections.

If anything went wrong in her life, she blamed my family, even though we lived in Michigan and she was in Arizona. We were accused of stealing her apartment key and anything else she couldn't find. I tried to take this all in stride because I knew she was not herself anymore. No longer was this the behavior of the Mother who had raised me.

During these displays of irrational behavior, part of me felt hurt and rejected and another part let it roll off. If I hadn't known Mother was suffering from some sort of dementia, I would have been devastated by her comments and actions. When she turned down my father's picture, part of me cried out on the inside, *That's my father, please don't dishonor him this way. I love him. Put that picture back up. I'm offended by what you are doing.*

These were natural emotions, of course, and I allowed myself to feel them. At the same time, I quickly realized Mother was out of touch. I knew that she loved my father, but her mind had misplaced who Daddy was to us. Memory of him had receded to some shadowy place in her mind. She was not expressing her real feelings. These were the actions and feelings of an irrational, illogical person. Realizing this, I was able to calm myself with a further acceptance of her thinking as no longer sensible, reasonable, clearheaded, or normal. If I had continued thinking she was in her right mind, I would have been crushed by many of her comments. I realized, when dealing with an Alzheimer victim, I had to put aside responses I had spent a lifetime building. New responses had to be acted out on my part in keeping with a loud understanding that Mother was no longer sane as we understand that term.

14

Intrinsic Worth and a Little History

So far I've painted a picture of my mother as she moved deeper into the abyss of Alzheimer's disease, but I can't let a disease be what defined her as a person. There was so much more to her as a woman created and valued by God. All humans have intrinsic worth simply from the fact that they are miraculously conceived, knit in their mother's womb, and born into this world. Psalm 139:14 attests that we are *"...fearfully and wonderfully made...,"* that God carefully formed us and wove us while we were in the secret of the womb. God knows us, understands us, and is intimately acquainted with all our ways. Every life has value.

My mother, Doris Marguerite (Dixon) Brown, was born September 8, 1913. The year 2013 would mark her 100th birthday if she were still alive. She was the second child of three, having an older brother, Don, and a younger brother, Richard. From her youth, she had many friends and enjoyed life. But sadly, by the time she was thirteen, her parents had grown apart and were divorced. In her diary, she never spoke of the divorce or the pain it must have caused her. I have heard that she and her father were close. She never personally spoke to me about what he was like, and as far as my memory goes, I only recall meeting him once.

We are all complex yet fragile beings, and the events of our early lives affect us for good or bad. Many people have scars from their childhood, but what we do with them as adults is the difference between a life of lemons or one of lemonade. Mother chose lemonade, even though I know her depths carried lemons throughout her life on several levels.

Her popularity as a teenager was clear from her diary as she spoke of many friends, especially among boys. If the term "guy magnet" had been in style, she would have qualified. There was one special boyfriend she mentioned during her late high school and college life. Interestingly, he suddenly disappeared from the pages of her journal and the next thing I knew, my father was in the picture as her favored date.

My father, Ralph E. Brown, met my mother on a train. She was seated next to him, and as the journey continued, he fell asleep. Slowly his head bobbed until it found a soft place to rest on her shoulder. Although this presented an awkward situation, unsure of how to handle it, she allowed him to doze there. I can only imagine their faces when he awoke. Hers with a hmmm…, what do you have to say for yourself look, raised eyebrows but a hint of amusement in her dancing brown eyes. His face flushed with embarrassment as he muffled an "I'm so sorry" explanation. What may have begun as an awkward moment led to a relationship that lasted forty years, until his death.

Mother attended the University of Kansas for two years after high school. She majored in geology, but her studies were cut short with her marriage and a move out of state. A number of years passed before they had children. During this time, there were several moves including Colorado and Texas, where I was eventually born. Without time to integrate into a community, and without children to tend, she took a job as a telephone operator. She once told me in passing that she never told my father about that job. How odd, I thought, that you could live with someone and not tell them where you were working or that you were working at all.

My father was a hard worker and provided well for our family, but his work took him away from home for three or four nights a week while I was growing up. He was a manager, and later, a district manager for McCrory stores, what we called five and dime stores in those days. When he left that line of work, he tried real estate and financial counseling.

I think my mother felt lonely much of her life. When at home, which was usually weekends, Daddy would be found either listening to sports on the radio, reading the Wall Street Journal, or later when we purchased a television, watching sports. I don't think there was a baseball team he didn't like. Mother missed Daddy and was lonely during the week while he was gone. On weekends she longed to do something fun with my father. Daddy, on the other hand, came home each weekend exhausted from travel and hard work and just wanted a quiet place to retreat.

Mother often withdrew to her room. There was an underlying melancholy beneath her positive, smiling demeanor which gave me a mixed message growing up. In her elderly years, I asked her about it, and she admitted that she had been unhappy but felt it was important to appear cheerful for the sake of others. While it made me sad to hear this, it gave me a better understanding of her life and how she dealt with the persistent ache in her heart.

Probably the most painful incident I witnessed was an evening when she and my father had planned to attend a Christmas ball at the country club. Mother loved parties. I remember her long flowing mauve gown, the white gloves, and an almost giddy expression on her face. Even with that, she looked regal as her eyes danced in delight. She was going to a party that she had looked forward to for months. Just the right dress, hours imagining the conversational chatter over dinner, seeing all the other gowns, the feeling of swirling in the arms of her husband as they glided over the dance floor. They had attended many club parties, but this was the social event of the year.

Waiting for Daddy, who was tied up doing inventory for his business, she watched for him through the window, anticipating his arrival. Then the call came. Her lip quivered. I watched as her eyes dulled over and a silent tear escaped from their pools. With a quiet goodbye, the phone resigned itself back in the cradle. Head down, without a word, Mother slipped into her bedroom and quietly closed the door. A muffled wail of anguish was all I heard as her unused gown now lay crumpled on the floor. She crawled under the covers in hopes of quick sleep to drown out the pain in her heart. Daddy had to work late, and they wouldn't be attending the ball after all. She had experienced other disappointments, but this time it broke something in her spirit. I still feel a knot in my stomach and sorrow when I remember the tears she wanted to hide from me as she ran into her room. I knew her tears were inconsolable.

Each one of us has done things we later regret. Although Daddy had taken my mother to many parties over the years, this particular evening was trumped by the urgent demands of work. While I don't know whether my father ever realized the hurt his choice brought to my mother that evening, I have noticed it was not the norm for couples in his generation to freely communicate personal feelings. Today is a different generation, and many women have grown bolder and learned how to communicate their feelings, and many men have learned to be better listeners and to share their feelings as well. I believe in his later years my father would have been very sorry to know how he had wounded my mother. He had a soft heart but sometimes lacked the capacity to give what he didn't have.

It's important in any relationship to understand that people can sometimes only give what they have been given. Our years growing up are meant to equip us with the tools we need to carry into the next generation. Sadly, many people are short changed in that area. I know my mother forgave him for his shortcomings. She was not one to hold a grudge. Compassion became the equalizer.

Someone once told me that the way you know you have forgiven someone is when you think of them, and your emotions are a flat line. I like that thought. Forgiveness

96

doesn't mean what the person did was right. It means that you have released them from any retribution or need to punish them. In essence, by freeing them, you are freeing yourself. You no longer feel the need to reprove the person. When you think of them, you offer compassion from the heart. Just as Jesus said from the cross, *"...Father forgive them; for they do not know what they are doing. . . "* (Lk.23:34), so we can be forgiving as well.

15
A Model of High Character

Mother had always been a model of decorum in every situation. I use the word decorum because it means to do whatever is proper, to show good taste in behavior, speech, and dress, to be polite. My mother's life represented quality in character and behavior. This is the woman I knew and loved. Yes, she had disappointments in life, some searing her heart, but she chose to look on the bright side and always had a positive word for every situation. She often said, "If you can't say something nice, Betsy, don't say anything at all."

Proverbs 31:28 says, *"Her children rise up and bless her. . . ."* Yes, I could rise up and bless my mother, and I can think of much for which to praise her. She had a heart of mercy. As we talked one day about spiritual gifts, she asked me what spiritual gift I thought God had given her.

"Mother, I believe God has given you the gift of mercy. You have devoted so many years to steadfastly taking care of friends and family members who lay sick or dying." Just recently, she had taken me with her to visit Esther, a friend who was recuperating from an operation.

Endurance, perseverance, and long suffering were very real in Mother's life experience. With the loss of her father through divorce, she experienced a difficult home life as she and her mother raised her little brother and her niece. Add to that, disappointments in her marriage and her own mother later succumbing to dementia. She was no stranger to hardship. Perhaps, today her mother's dementia might have been called Alzheimer's disease too. Mother rose to the occasion and laid down her life to serve her mother's needs in her latter years, even moving back to Kansas to help where needed.

Some years after her mother's passing, she watched as my father slowly died a long and grueling death from cancer. She chose to keep him at home to the end. Through all this, she made herself available to any friend who endured sickness or suffering. Mother was there to help as God enabled her. With each difficulty that life presented, she always maintained composure, a positive attitude, and a soft heart. I'm sure God honored her for that.

With that as background, to hear my mother saying negative things, as Alzheimer's ravaged her mind, seemed out of context to her personality, to the mother I knew. Listening as she accused me unrealistically, talked to pictures, and just plain didn't make sense, required quite an adjustment in my perspective.

The Mirror

Along with her disturbance with pictures of my family and my father, another unusual fixation that captured Mother involved the bathroom mirror. Her bathroom in the retirement home was small but had a flat mirror spanning the wall and an adjacent mirror on the bathroom cabinet. Mother began telling me about the woman who lived in her bathroom and how troubling she found her.

"That girl is in my bathroom again! I just can't use my bathroom with her in there. I wish she would leave me alone." Her bitterness was palpable. It became stressful for her to use her apartment bathroom with "that girl" watching her every move. Her uneasiness over this situation soon made it impossible for her to use her bathroom at all. As a result, she began using a public restroom in her building. "That girl," the image of herself in the mirror, could not be explained or understood in any rational sense.

When she calmed down after one episode and her breathing returned to normal, I inquired, "Mother, do you realize 'that girl' is just you in the mirror?"

"Well, yes I know who it is," she sheepishly concurred, but in the next breath she referred to her as "that girl" and clearly became bothered once again. In a short moment of clarity, some part of her brain had shifted and she recognized reality. But just as quickly, her mind lost the flicker of light, the momentary spark, and returned to the shadows of Alzheimer's.

I'm not sure why "that girl" was such an enemy. Perhaps seeing herself age was more than she could emotionally cope with. Maybe it was simply a result of the obvious brain deterioration she experienced. Perhaps someday, scientists will be able to more fully explain what goes on in the mind of victims of Alzheimer's disease.

Frustration in Communication

I think the hardest thing in watching Mother's mind slip away was dealing with her absolute insistence that she was perfectly fine, that not a thing was wrong with her. She usually became irate if I even hinted that she suffered any memory loss. Since I'm very truth oriented and thrive on clear communication in relationships, especially when problems are involved, I often felt frustrated not being able to talk with Mother about the changes that were so evident in her life. If only she would have said, "Yes, I've noticed I don't remember as well as I used to," or "I'm concerned about the strange things I hear myself saying." But these things were all kept in the dark, in a secret place hidden away from the present reality.

Pertinent dialogue, explanations, working through issues, agreement, touching of souls, all the things that make us human had been expunged from my mother's brain. Normal conversation was a thing I longed for. I wanted my real mother back. I missed our engaging conversations about everything from family to politics. This person was not my mother. Something was seriously wrong. Something valuable, beyond worth, had been stolen from her and from our relationship. From me!

If she was aware of the changes taking place in her behavior, she didn't give me a hint. When I alluded to her confusion or forgetfulness in any way, she became defensive and firmly told me she was not crazy. I quickly agreed that, of course, she wasn't crazy. I wondered if she had any awareness that her behavior was odd. Was she conflicted at all by her present actions and thinking? If she was, I didn't know about it.

In all of these beginning changes, there were times I felt acutely conflicted and confused. At times, it was difficult to pass by her comments, her odd behavior. Showing grace to someone who doesn't communicate is a challenge on any level, but I wrestled with how it works with a person who is losing their personhood. While truth and honesty are very important to me, we had crossed a chasm into unknown territory where these qualities were now skewed into an alternate reality. Did I have times of conflict in my soul about this? Yes, I did. How did God want me to respond? I decided it was only by His grace that I would be able to proceed. I did not have the inner strength to deal with this situation on my own. His grace, His strength, His wisdom, these would accompany me as we explored the depths together.

16
Assisted Living

After Mother had lived in the retirement home for six months, we received a call from the administrator. She advised us that they felt it would be in Mother's best interest to move her to their assisted living wing. It would be an identical apartment to the one she now occupied, but added services would be provided. These would include laundry, bathing, dressing assistance, housekeeping help, and dispensing of her medications. By now, we clearly understood that Mother was no longer able to handle the responsibilities of living independently. Upon conferring with Cynthia and Bill, we all quickly agreed this move sounded like a good idea. I'm sure we gave a collective sigh of relief with this decision. Knowing Mother's needs would be more fully met assuaged many of our concerns. It was agreed that I would make the trip to Arizona to help her move again.

Upon arriving, I carefully brought up the subject that the retirement home felt they could better serve her if she moved to another floor of the building. I tried to help her understand some of the extra benefits that would be provided. At first, she opposed another move, and I understood her feelings. No move is easy and she had already moved once that year, but as an incentive I promised her "that girl" wouldn't move with her. That seemed to give her enough relief to gain an affirmative answer.

The move went well and was fairly uneventful. Same building, different floor. The first thing we did, after settling her into her new apartment, was to purchase some pretty pink, flowered wrapping paper which we hung over the bathroom mirrors. Now "that girl" should no longer pose a problem. While this brought some relief, Mother remained convinced "that girl" still lurked somewhere in the room. At least she no longer saw her and agreed to use her own bathroom again.

Personal Appearance

Mother had always been a beautiful woman, elegant and sophisticated in appearance. For years she had worn her long salt and pepper hair in braids across the top of her head. Short permed curls swept softly off her forehead. Such a unique and attractive hair style, it drew the attention and admiration of many over the years. Her appearance was nothing short of striking. However, a year before her first move, she had decided to have her hair cut short. Perhaps reaching to brush and braid her hair had become tedious in her elderly years. Or perhaps she had simply forgotten how to braid her hair. My guess would be the latter.

Without the use of her bathroom mirror, now covered with wall paper, Mother's personal appearance began to diminish. Her short hairdo flattened between beauty appointments, and she had given up combing it herself. I struggled getting used to seeing her with short hair in the first place, and it took months for the hairdresser to fix it in a comely style. The aides helped some, but in the area of grooming hair, they lacked expertise. The first time I saw her unkempt and with hair badly in need of washing shocked me. I soon learned that she had not been showing up for her beauty appointments. I asked the aides to start taking her each week because she could no longer remember to go on her own.

As her Alzheimer's progressed, she lost all interest in her appearance, including how she dressed. It was reported to me that she showed up in the dining room wearing only her blouse and a slip on one occasion. The assistant discreetly led her back to her room. Mother didn't seem particularly disturbed but did forget to return for her meal.

Confusion

Every move has its downside, and regrettably, in no time, Mother experienced measurable confusion finding her new apartment. She had previously been on the third floor and was now in an identical apartment on the second floor. With her new assisted living apartment on a different floor of the building, she had significant difficulty adjusting to her new location. Her habit was to return to her old apartment. There, she banged on the door, insisting that her family was locked inside, and she should be let in immediately. I can only imagine how emotionally distraught and angry she must have been, thinking she was locked out of her own home. And it must have been equally distressing to the person who now lived in her old room, having a woman banging on his door at uninvited times of the day. Fortunately, in this part of the building, doors could be locked at the discretion of the tenant, so she couldn't just walk in.

We continued to receive reports from Carl periodically. He explained that Mother had visited a friend in another apartment. It was raining outside so when she finished the visit, she phoned him. "Carl, will you come and pick me up? It's raining outside and I don't have my umbrella with me."

"Where are you, Doris?" Carl puzzled.

"Well, I'm in room 319," she stiffly retorted as though Carl should have known.

Hearing the room number, he knew she was still in her building and wouldn't have to go outside to return to her apartment, so he patiently suggested, "Why don't you just walk on back to your room, Doris, since you haven't left the building?"

"You don't even care if I get wet!" she snapped, slamming down the phone.

Mother's life had become terribly frustrating to her. What made perfect, logical sense in her mind seemed to be challenged at every turn by the alternate, yet true reality of those around her. Her anxiety level remained high, and restlessness hounded her day and night.

From her point of view, it was perplexing, if not overwhelming, to constantly have people question and doubt what she said. Most people are bothered when corrected more than once on an issue, but to have your lifestyle become one where almost everything you say is brought into question, must have been disconcerting, if not devastating.

Wandering

Each week brought new challenges to Mother's disorientation as to which apartment was hers. One week, I spoke to her on the phone from Michigan as she related, "They've moved me down to the first floor, Betsy."

"They have?" I asked in surprise. Of course, my mind became a jumble of thoughts as I wondered what on earth was going on now. She had originally been on the third floor in the retirement section, now resided on the second floor but was claiming they had moved her to the first floor. This news had me baffled since the staff had always been diligent in keeping me updated regarding Mother's needs and any changes that were made. I had not been informed of any further moves.

"Why did they move you?" I questioned.

"I don't know why they moved me. There's a sick man in my room now. He's in bed, and I don't like the situation one bit!" Her tone was both befuddled and annoyed.

I couldn't imagine what she was talking about. Immediately upon hanging up, I dialed the administrator. I didn't know what to think of this turn of events. Quickly, the mystery unraveled. Apparently Mother frequently wandered at night. In her confusion, upon returning to her apartment from dinner, she forgot to take the elevator to her floor. Since the layout of each floor was identical, she ended up walking into the room just below her apartment. The first floor was also assisted living and all doors were left unlocked, so unlike the third floor room she used to try to open, she had easy access to any room on this floor. Easy access can be a good thing for the employees, but for one bewildered man, it was not so good.

Mother repeated her trek to the wrong room on several more occasions. Startled by seeing a strange woman in his room, the man who lived there called the aides to usher her out each time. Much to his frustration, Mother insisted he was trespassing. How baffling this must have been to Mother who was completely convinced that someone was in her apartment. Her mind must have swirled in confusion, yet she firmly believed what she perceived. Someone was violating her space.

17
Carl's Frustration

Carl's calls to us came more frequently as Mother
became more adept at hiding things. "Betsy, we can't
find your mother's purse anywhere," he related one evening
on the phone. "We've looked everywhere. It's not even in
the back of the kitchen cupboard or in the linen closet under
the towels this time. Her wallet and checkbook are in it, so
how should she pay for her beauty appointment?"

As a devoted friend, I sensed Carl's frustration as he told
me about what had transpired the last few times he had asked
her to go out to dinner. He would call to remind her an hour
before picking her up, only to arrive and find she had either
eaten already or was sitting in the dining room ordering.
Sometimes, he didn't find out she had eaten until her dinner
arrived at the restaurant. Feeling full, Mother would pick at
her food with no recollection that she had eaten dinner less
than an hour ago.

The Baby

Mother's fixation on pictures continued as an important part of her everyday life. She found a picture of a darling baby girl in a magazine. Pleased this baby had come to live with her, she often spoke of her with endearing terms.

"Betsy, I'm just so tickled this baby has come to live with me. I'm enjoying her so much." I now heard about the baby with each phone call. Then one day Mother announced, "Betsy, I'm pregnant!"

I paused, speechless. A quiet prayer...*how do I handle this news?* This one took the cake. After a short pause to think of how to respond, I tentatively asked, "What makes you think you're pregnant, Mother?"

"Well, you know!" she sheepishly replied.

Normally an early riser, she began sleeping in to take care of the baby. She was quick to agree that it was unusual for a woman her age to be with child but insisted it was true.

Interestingly, it seemed that each story she told had some shred of truth or some semblance to reality if I looked for it. Mother, in this case, had been putting on some weight. She wasn't fat, but was bigger in the waist from eating more. Apparently, when her clothes began to fit tighter, her mind computed that she must be pregnant. The thought may have also been connected with the time she spent focusing on her picture of a baby. So, if I looked at the announcement from the perspective of her reality, it seemed plausible for her to think she was pregnant.

Hard Decisions

About this time, Bill was preparing to leave on a business trip to Arizona and had asked me to come along. We planned to stay in a nice resort and spend some time relaxing as he only had a few seminars to present during the week. Before leaving, we received a timely call from the assisted living administrator. She would like to sit down with us and evaluate Mother's situation. Uh oh....

I felt I knew what was coming. So much for the vacation and lounging by the pool! I began to do some serious praying. I diligently sought God's will that week for my mother's situation. Was it time to move her to Michigan? She had only been in the assisted living unit for a few months, but I had to admit, her situation was rapidly deteriorating. We all realized that, but what were we to do? Should she live with us? What were our choices? After she had visited us the previous Christmas, I had sworn I could never move her to our home. It had not been a victorious week for any of us.

The whole family had been in our home for the holidays and it was a stressful time constantly having to monitor Mother's every move. Everything was in slow motion. Dressing, bathing, using the facilities, all took volumes of time. She also spent hours in the kitchen playing in the sink. Rinsing and stacking the dishes, then more rinsing and stacking. It reminded me of the times our children enjoyed playing in the water as preschoolers, except Mother didn't have to stand on a stool. More than once, I caught her drying the dirty dishes in the dishwasher and putting them in the cupboard. I tried not to think of the implications of that. I just reminded myself that we were all family.

It was never Mother's wish to be a burden. She was doing the best she could. In her simple way, she thought she was helping in the kitchen. Everyone likes to feel useful. I couldn't be too hard on her. There is a great deal of dignity in being able to maintain independence. As we grow older, we all dread losing our freedom. Mother had lost her home, her car, her ability to care for herself, and now needed constant supervision.

Another factor in thinking of Mother moving in with us was our concern as to how she would treat Mike who was then eight years old. Where Mother used to be gentle and sweet with children, she now showed signs of harsh intolerance toward Mike. He was a very agreeable and compliant child who enjoyed cooperating and fitting in with family. More than once I had seen the puzzled and hurt look on his little face when Grandma had blamed him unrealistically for things he wouldn't have thought of doing. When Bill, Cynthia, and I talked that week, we all agreed that moving Mother to our home would not be the best long term solution.

As I prayed, another factor laid heavily on my heart. Carl, who had been my second angel, the first being the kind elderly lady on my first flight to Arizona, had recently made the decision to move to Colorado. At eighty years old he had been thinking about his own mortality. Who would take care of him if he fell ill? After much thought, he had decided it would be best for him to be closer to his own family. The move would take place in two months.

What would Mother do without Carl? In truth, what would we all do without Carl? He had been such a blessing in her life, phoning every day, visiting her every evening, taking her to the symphony, out to dinner, to visit friends, to the store, and to appointments. Who would visit Mother and take her out and keep us informed if Carl moved? While we heartily agreed this was a prudent move for him, at the same time, we sensed a real loss about to happen in Mother's life. We faced a dilemma. The best thing I know to do when faced with decisions is to pray. Jesus is Lord, the One who has mapped out the plans, the course to take. He would supply. He would provide. Proverbs 16:3 says, *Commit your works to the Lord and your plans will be established.*

Key Principle #9 - Pray diligently for every need. Sometimes, needs all piled up at once. Facing them without calling upon God was unthinkable. Leaning on Him for every decision was the only way I knew to walk in victory. Through prayer, I had the privilege of seeing God move in many ways on Mother's behalf. He cared deeply for her. We were so thankful for His provision and were comforted by His answers. Proverbs 16:9 offers the promise, *"The mind of man plans his way, but the Lord directs his steps."* Such words of reassurance and comfort.

116

18
Time for a Decision

Upon arriving in Arizona, I made an appointment to speak with Sheri, the assisted living administrator. I quickly realized she had called me in for exactly what I had imagined. As she reviewed how she perceived Mother's condition, she indicated she felt Mother needed more supervision and care than they could provide even with assisted living. Her only suggestion was that we hire someone to come in and be with Mother a number of hours during the day and evening. We considered her suggestion, but it seemed like too much for us to hire more help for Mother. Living across the country, how would we be able to keep up with all that would involve? Although her present facility wasn't enough now, the next step would be a nursing home, and we didn't feel she was at that point either. She was not bed ridden.

"Your mother seems very lonely and disoriented, Betsy. We see her wandering day and night, and she spends much of her time talking to the help at the desk," Sheri explained. "She's such a dear, sweet person. We are concerned about her spending so much time alone." I began to see what I already suspected; it was time to move her to Michigan. God was clearly directing our steps.

Some might ask why we didn't move Mother to Michigan sooner. She obviously needed help. In retrospect, I wondered that too. Then I remember that she had been in the retirement home less than a year, including the move to assisted living. While her early symptoms came on slowly, in the past year they had increased more rapidly, and many symptoms came at the same time. Living a distance away and unaware that Mother had Alzheimer's disease definitely slowed our decision process. Alzheimer's was not well known in the 1980's, and not much was written about it. When I later began to look for books, I found only a few to read. The internet was just starting to gain popularity, so even that would not have helped. We didn't have a personal computer until sometime in the 1990's, long after she was gone. Today that sounds impossible, but much has changed in technology in the past twenty years.

Mother loved Arizona, and I had tried to honor her wish to stay there as long as possible. She still had definite feelings and opinions, even though she no longer functioned like a normal person. Dignity is important for anyone, and there was a fine balance between helping her and allowing her to be as responsible as possible for her own life. Each transition was difficult for both of us. I felt awkward taking over Mother's life and making so many decisions for her. Those who have walked in similar paths understand this.

On one of my previous trips to Arizona, I had visited a couple of nursing homes in an effort to see if there would be any way we could keep her there longer. Even in the early stages, the idea of having her so far away bothered me, but I wanted to check out all the available options.

The facilities were all very caring and the patients lovingly tended to, and I was impressed with the happy faces of the people. The majority of the patients socialized with one another in their rooms, in sitting areas, and in the halls. One nursing home had an Alzheimer section. Within the Alzheimer unit were four separate areas. Each one had a gate operated by the nurses. The sections of this particular nursing home ranged from mild Alzheimer patients to those in the last stages of the disease.

"How do you keep the patients from leaving their area?" I asked the guide as she punched in some buttons to open the gate.

"Oh, that's not a problem. The gates open to a code that only the nurses know in the mild area, but in the advanced Alzheimer section, we just keep the code written on the wall. The patients aren't cognizant enough in their reasoning to figure it out even when it's written down," she explained. Apparently the numbers on the wall were no more than gibberish to them. There was no brain connection between the coded numbers and the lock on the door. It reminded me of when my mother couldn't figure out how to run the washing machine not many months prior.

The clanging of the gate closing behind us in the Alzheimer's unit sent a chill through me. While I understood their reason for keeping the gates locked, it jolted me to think of Mother in a facility like this. Alzheimer's patients habitually wander. They sometimes roam outside and get lost with no understanding of how to return. But still, this facility seemed more like a prison than a retirement home. The thought of Mother living behind bars made me shudder. It was difficult to imagine she might eventually need this kind of attention. I prayed God would provide an alternative answer.

Before we had left for our so called business trip/vacation to Arizona, I had asked the Lord to help me explore housing options for people with Alzheimer's in our town. Where would Mother live if we moved her to Michigan? I knew she wasn't ready for a nursing home, and the other facilities in our town were similar to where she now resided. I was stumped, but I sensed that God was not and that, at the right time, He would provide for Mother's growing needs.

If left to my own resources, the future looked daunting, but with God, all things are possible. He is unrelenting in His desire to unfold His plans for our lives. His purposes, while obscure to us at times, always ended in hope. I found comfort in Jeremiah 29:11, *"For I know the plans that I have for you, declares the Lord, plans for welfare and not for calamity, to give you a future and a hope."* Indeed God had a plan and it was about to unfold.

God's Provision

Several days before our trip, I happened to be reading a local weekly paper called the Shopper's Guide. I wasn't thinking about Mother at the time, but an ad for an adult foster care home caught my eye. I knew that there were homes of this type for mentally handicapped people, but I had never heard of one like the one described in the paper. It seemed to be a home for elderly people who needed special care. I read with curiosity that they had an opening for a lady. With my interest peaked, I phoned for an appointment. The address was in a nice section of town, and I planned a visit that afternoon.

As I drove down the broad, tree lined street in the quiet residential neighborhood, I thought the homes looked comfortable and the neighborhood friendly. The foster care home was located on a corner, and I soon learned it had previously been owned by a local doctor. The outside was welcoming with its wide entry walk and neatly arranged bushes and flowers along the house. The location was perfect, almost behind our church and just a few miles from our home, which although on the other side of town, was not far. Nothing in our town of 10,000 is really very far away. Bill used to joke with our California friends when we moved to Michigan that we had a rush "minute"...not a rush hour. When asked how far he was from work, he explained it was five minutes...if he walked.

The moment I entered this lovely ranch style house, I knew this was God's answer to my prayer. I loved this beautiful and tastefully decorated home. The large living room just inside the front door was full of light and connected to a lovely dining area where the ladies sat together for their meals. Pleasant smells of dinner being prepared wafted to greet me. I pictured Mother enjoying home cooking again, chatting with new friends. Her bedroom would be located at the front of the house with a large window for fresh air and light. Spacious, yet cozy looking, I was sure she could be comfortable there as I imagined several pieces of her furniture in place. Her bed and dresser would fit nicely, and I could envision her sitting in her beloved rocking chair reading and nodding off as was her custom.

Run by a caring middle aged couple, they told me their motto: "Only kind words spoken here." Upon meeting the other ladies who were living there, I quickly realized this was a place of contentment and peace. Mother would get lots of attention, and her growing needs would be well tended.

The home had a warm, personal feel. It was small enough that she would have minimal adjustment to finding things, yet she would have the privacy of her own room. I knew she would like it. The caretakers were obviously hard workers and ran a very efficient, orderly home. Fay, the owner, had an easy smile. I liked her immediately. I felt we connected as we spoke of our mutual desire for Mother's care. Her own older sister had suffered from early onset Alzheimer's, and Fay had taken care of her until she passed away. Fay definitely had a soft heart for those afflicted with this disease.

Since Bill and I planned to leave for Arizona the next week, we told Fay that we would get back to her after we spoke to Mother. We also needed to hear the administrator's concerns before we rushed headlong into another decision. I didn't feel hurried to reserve a place at that time. I was sure that if this home was God's provision, a room would be there when we needed it. This almost seemed odd when I later thought of it but, at the time, I felt such faith rise in me as I considered how God had directed me to this location. I was convinced God's plans would not be thwarted if this was where Mother was to live.

I had already looked at one other possible location in our area and felt it was dark and somewhat dismal. Mother enjoyed lots of light. The room they had offered was tiny, almost like a closet. I didn't have a good feeling about it upon leaving. No, the well lit home on the corner in the charming neighborhood would be perfect. God had surely led me to it. I did not know such housing existed until I had "coincidentally" read about it in the paper.

A special verse comes to mind as I remember this home and my decision to wait. Proverbs 3:5-6, *"Trust in the Lord with all your heart and do not lean on your own understanding. In all your ways acknowledge Him, and He will make your paths straight."* Seventeen times the phrase "trust in the Lord" is used in the Bible. Mother and I were about to enter new, unknown paths, uncharted territory that would make that verse a reality in ways I hadn't imagined. This was the beginning of meeting God at every turn.

Photos

Bottom Row: Carmen, Mike, Mother Middle Row: Laurie, Kim, Betsy, Top Row: Lou and Bill

Cynthia, Mother, Betsy, Daughters Laurie and Kim, Aunt Betty

Ralph and Doris dressed for a ball they did get to attend

Bill and Betsy, Christmas 2011

126

Mike, and Grandma Brown with shorter hair, attending Grandparent's day at Mike's school. Alzheimer's has changed Mother's appearance.

Carl, Mother's dear and faithful friend

Kim, Betsy and Mother with Mother's first great grandchild, Erika

Mother in her elderly years before Alzheimer's

Mother in her younger years

Betsy, age 3 and Mother, in her early thirties

Mother as a teenager. No wonder boys enjoyed her company.

Cynthia's husband, Gary, Betsy and Cynthia

One of our last photos of Mother with latter stage Alzheimer's, still a classy lady

How I like to remember Mother, happily ready for a good party

Betsy's father, Ralph

Easter, 2011. Bill and Betsy on the left, Laurie in white in the front row, Kim and her husband John in the back row; Mike, on the far right, back row and his wife, Katie, with baby Jacob in the front row. Also, 7 of Mother's 8 grandchildren. Only Erika is missing. Mother would have been proud.

19
Planning Another Move

One of the things I learned about dealing with a person with Alzheimer's is that you have to be ready to respond to change, and it often comes quickly. Having talked to the administrator early in our week in Arizona, it was confirmed that Mother now needed more care than their facility could provide. Midweek in our work\pleasure trip, Carl boldly approached me and suggested that we pack Mother up and take her with us when we flew back home at the end of the week. At first, I couldn't imagine such an impulsive decision. I had planned to return to Arizona in a month and do the process more slowly. Although we were now convinced we needed to move Mother to Michigan, the thought of doing it immediately caught me by surprise and seemed a little overwhelming.

However, as Bill and I entertained the idea, it began to sound plausible. It would save me another trip With Bill there with me, his strength and support would be encouraging as we prepared Mother and launched into the many arrangements that would have to be made. After discussing the possibility with him and Cynthia, we all agreed it did sound like a good idea. So, we began the chore of preparing yet another move for Mother.

Since I had not signed papers to secure a place for Mother to stay in Michigan, she would have to be in our home for at least a few days. That would be do-able. I felt sure that the adult foster care home would still be our best option, and I felt at peace that God would go before us to save her a room.

As we sought the Lord about the awesome task of moving Mother across the country with only three day's notice, He reminded me of Proverbs 16:3, *"Commit your works to the Lord, and your plans will be established."* Clearly, the Lord moved to direct and establish our steps that week as we made the necessary preparations for Mother to move from Arizona to Michigan in record time. Having time with God as the first priority each day, I claimed Matthew 6:33, *"But seek first His kingdom and His righteousness; and all these things will be added to you."* Truly, I needed the "all these things" part added to our week, and indeed I received them.

With one day of phone calls, I lined up the moving van and the auctioneer. I made arrangements with Mother's bank, talked with her investment agents, canceled her phone, talked to the Post Office, and made countless other provisions for the move. The Lord even provided her a plane ticket on our flight home with a seat next to ours. With three day's notice, I considered that a miracle.

The next two days, I sorted through her remaining possessions, once again deciding what to take and what to sell. Since I had moved her twice before, I was beginning to feel like a pro. Stacks of boxes and loose items lay in piles throughout the apartment according to what would accompany her to Michigan and what would be sold the next week in an auction. It was a daunting task as I considered how little could be taken on this move. All of her precious items, her silver, china, jewelry, and pictures would have to go into storage in our home. Although I knew she wouldn't be using them again, I also knew that she wanted the family to have these things when she eventually went to live in her eternal home with the Lord. Having some of her valued things there would comfort us and help us remember her.

Since this was the last kitchen she would have, I gave away almost everything: pots and pans, silverware, and odds and ends of utensils. Nostalgic thoughts washed over me as I cleared out the remains of that room. It seemed a final statement that Mother would never be a homemaker again, never cook a meal again, never wash dishes and tidy up the kitchen. So much of a woman's role, especially women of her generation, was tied up in the kitchen. Memories of meals she had prepared over the years, her willingness to entertain family and friends, sweet conversations we had enjoyed around the table, and even at the sink doing dishes, so many things revolved around the kitchen. For Mother, this was the end of another era. I guess it kind of snuck up on us. Even in her retirement apartment, she had a kitchen where we had breakfast together.

Actually, one of the first hints I had that Mother was not quite herself had happened on a visit a couple years prior to this. We had arrived expecting to be served a nice meal as was her custom and were surprised when dinner consisted of hot dogs and canned beans. My conjecture today would be that she was already forgetting how to cook at that time. Now we were closing up her kitchen one last time, never to be opened again.

When the moving company representative came to list what items to take, I realized too late that I should have taken Mother out of the room while we talked. With her remaining in the room, of course, she wanted a say about her possessions. According to her, everything should be packed and moved to Michigan. This made conversation difficult because I knew only a few things could be taken this time. Left behind would be much of her living room and bedroom furniture. There simply wouldn't be room in her new location.

She became so troubled by the process that I finally suggested Carl and Bill take her out to dinner so that decisions involving the movers could be expedited. In her confused state, Mother found it especially hard to watch her personal belongings diminish once again and to sense the further termination of her independence and control of her life. However, part of me wondered if she really had any idea what was happening. Her responses were focused on the immediate activity, changes she observed happening in her apartment. Her nest was again being ruffled and the mother hen was understandably stirred up.

It was sad because we knew that this would be the hardest move yet. The most difficult part would be telling Mother because we knew she wouldn't understand at all. Sadly, she was beyond the point of being able to make decisions. With God's help, we could do this.

When we broached the subject this time about a move, we first asked if she would agree to go, yet it seemed more like an ultimatum. There were no other viable options at this point; but to maintain her dignity, we wanted her involved in the process, hoping against hope that she would agree. It was hard making decisions which we knew she wouldn't want. Honoring my mother in the midst of Alzheimer's was important to me and our family, even when we were aware of how unrealistic her desires were. It was a fine line with precarious tension at times.

We gave her all the logical reasons for this move as we had for others, but we had to remember her mind was further compromised and clearly wasn't working logically. After explaining that Carl planned to move to Colorado, leaving her virtually friendless, she frantically cried, "Nobody told me Carl was moving!"

Of course, Carl, Bill, and I had all told her numerous times but she had no memory of these conversations. In her mind Carl would always be there. How sad to lose such a devoted friend.

One afternoon, as Mother and I took a break to sit by the apartment pool, she craned her neck to see the street. "I thought I just saw the moving van bringing Carl's things here."

I'm not sure she ever understood that Carl was moving to Colorado, not to her retirement home. I can only assume she heard us use the words "Carl, and move," but with her jumbled thinking, she put it in the context of him moving to her building. Her sweet innocence brought tears to my eyes as she looked for the van with such longing expectation. Even with part her mind gone, she still had hopes, still yearned for the familiar, the things in life that brought comfort. Dear Carl was surely one of those.

Mother remained unhappy about moving to Michigan. Sometimes she commented, "I'm never moving to Michigan; I like it here. Why do I have to move?" Then she would pick up a newspaper and become lost to our conversation as she commenced reading aloud. Convinced that she was capable of taking care of herself, she saw no reason why she should be uprooted once again.

Cooperating with God's Plan

If I had not seen God's hand so clearly, I, too, could have harbored serious doubts about the move. Mother had spent the past seventeen years in a warm climate. In our part of the country, we had to contend half the year with a cold, rainy, snowy climate. I read one time that Michigan has the third fewest days of sun per year in the U.S., so this move for Mother meant a completely different climate. In Michigan, we can go for weeks in the winter without seeing the sun.

Mother was also used to a large city. Ours was a small, agricultural community. Bill and I loved where we lived, the small town atmosphere, the distinct seasons, the feeling of safety, and the friendliness of the people. But from Mother's perspective, it made her feel cold to even think of Michigan. Her viewpoint was understandable.

To be honest, although I loved my mother, I grappled with the idea of her being back in my life full time after living hundreds of miles from each other for twenty five years. I was content with my life the way it was. Some drastic changes were on the horizon for all of us as I contemplated her living close to us in her present condition. The thought of the pending responsibility for an elderly parent while we were still raising a young son weighed heavily on my mind. Our daughters, Kim and Laurie, were in college, so they would not be available to share some of the responsibilities that lay ahead. We already led a busy life, involved in church work, home groups, school activities, athletic events, etc. Our calendar was full. I wasn't sure I was prepared for all the change, which turned out to be even greater than we knew. Although conflicted, our family loved my mother, and we truly wanted to be there for her. I know now it was absolutely the right thing to do, and although there were many sad times ahead, there were also some really sweet times that more than made up for them.

The Lord had some work to do in my heart to prepare me for what lay ahead. I realized my new life would take a lot of time and patience. As I prayed about the situation, the Lord revealed to me that I had a choice to make. I could resist this change and make myself and everyone around me miserable in the process, or I could trust God and believe that He had something good in it for me and my family: a new opportunity in God with the hope of seeing Him as never before...or a defeated time of hopeless misery. God was holding out a clear choice. After some wrestling, I made the decision to cooperate with Him as best I could, to trust Him to direct my path.

I've learned that making a clear decision to do the right thing and to have a "happy heart" is critical. We often told our children when they were growing up that obedience was this: When you're asked to do something, do it right away and with a happy heart. Well, I was about to find out that principle would work well in my life, too, as I cared for my mother.

20
Choices

Rarely do circumstances affect just one person. More likely, any given situation touches a number of lives. God had a plan and a purpose for each person in Mother's life. Mother's decline affected every member of our family in some way. Her disease influenced not only her but her friends, her caretaker, and her family.

Alert to God, I eagerly listened to discern what He wanted to teach me, what He wanted to build into my life as a result of my new and very different relationship with my mother. Looking at our situation in that light helped me to see the whole matter as an "Adventure in God." I learned to see life from a larger perspective as I trusted God to accomplish His purpose in my life and hers through the circumstances at hand.

I made a conscious choice to have this attitude while Mother remained alive and in our care. Only then would my joy, peace, and contentment stay intact. Romans 14:17 says, *"For the kingdom of God is not eating and drinking, but righteous, peace, and joy in the Holy Spirit."* The choice was mine each day to allow God to activate His kingdom in my life. I chose to believe that God loved both Mother and me and was working out His perfect plan. Isaiah 25:1 reveals, *"O Lord, You are my God; I will exalt You, I will give thanks to Your name; For You have worked wonders, Plans formed long ago, with perfect faithfulness."* I liked the thought that His plans were made with perfect faithfulness. All of His paths found their root in His abundant love for us. I believed that not only did this make a difference for my life, but what God was doing in me helped my mother accept and live her life to a fuller extent as well.

One evening I watched a woman on a Christian television program who shared how she had been in an accident that left her a paraplegic. As she recovered from some of her injuries, it began to sink in that without the use of her legs, she would be spending the rest of her life in a wheelchair. She would no longer be able to jump out of bed, take a walk, jog with a neighbor, or easily get around for errands. The changes in her life were overwhelming to consider. What could have turned into a bitter experience, turned to acceptance and expectation when she received a word from the Lord, "Do not despise the things I have allowed in your life." Those words changed her entire outlook. Because of this clear exhortation, no bitterness took root in her heart. Today, while limited physically, she lives a productive life emotionally, mentally, and spiritually. She chose to embrace her situation.

Contrast this with another woman I met at a conference. Her story was similar in that she was also confined to a wheelchair. The difference was her attitude. She was full of bitterness and shook her fist at God. How dare He ruin her life! Her eyes flashed with anger and resentment as she lamented her life condition. Her attitude had become so acidic that people felt uncomfortable around her. I personally looked for an escape from her negative spewing. A life that could have been a testimony of God's goodness in the midst of pain had become a depressing volcano of hate, an odious outpouring of pessimism.

A number of years ago, we had an older friend in California named Rusty who had severe breathing issues and had been confined to an iron lung for several years. Following her confinement, we ran into her at a Christian conference center when it was again safe for her to go out, although she still had to carry an oxygen tank to breathe normally. For all practical purposes, she was now able to live a normal life. Her eyes sparkled as she expressed the goodness of God during her time of incapacitation. I was stymied as to how she could have maintained her positive attitude while enduring such a tedious and disabling ailment. I asked her how she had passed the time while, in what seemed like, imprisonment in an iron lung. With an infectious smile, she explained that she had developed what she called an "Iron Lung Ministry" of prayer. During that season of her life, she had realized that God was offering her a choice. She could waste her endless hours feeling sorry for herself, or she could use them for kingdom purposes. She made a volitional decision to spend hours each day seeking the Lord in prayer by interceding for other people's needs. Not only that, but she expected to see Him move and to hear answers to her prayers. She became a powerful and effective intercessor. Through this outreach, her hope was restored. She had purpose. She felt God had actually allowed her to be confined for a greater purpose, a divine purpose.

While being restricted as a shut in herself, she never looked at it as a prison but rather as an opportunity. God impressed on her the idea of using this time productively to pray. Use of her physical body may have been stolen for a season, but God had higher purposes for her life and she was eager to cooperate with the task. For several years, she stormed the gates of heaven for the benefit of others. That, to me, is an example of a life well spent. What it all boils down to is this: Life is all about attitudes and choices. And the best choice is to allow Jesus to live His life in and through us.

Psalm 27:13-14 says, *"I would have despaired unless I had believed that I would see the goodness of the Lord in the land of the living. Wait for the Lord; Be strong, and let your heart take courage; Yes, wait for the Lord."*

We are a "now" generation. We want things to happen instantly, to change immediately without delay, and without any suffering involved. If there is a moment of pain or discomfort, we want out at once. But in reality, we often have to wait for God's best, and that usually takes time to grow and develop. Although it's not a Bible verse, I think God would likely say, *Do not despise the things I have allowed in your life. Count the cost, and realize I may be at work and ready to reveal a meaningful plan.*

While waiting for God to reveal His plan, we don't need to choose pouting or despair. Rather, we must choose to believe that He will faithfully perform His work in us and through us, knowing that the process often includes waiting. There is usually a cost, a choice to be made. We can take courage in knowing this is how He operates. He hasn't forgotten us. We walk by faith, not by sight.

During difficult times, and really all the time, life is about choices...choices... and more choices. One speaker put it this way. "I was asked to speak a eulogy for a man who was my mentor, a great man. I agreed but didn't know what to say. His wife gave me directions to their home in a mountain community. When I got to the town, I was still baffled. What could I say about this man who had changed my life? The final directions led me to my answer. As I turned to go up the mountain roads to where they lived, her directions said, 'When you come to the first fork in the road, take the higher road.' She repeated the same directions three more times. By the time I had made the last turn, I had my message. It was simple. It was the way my friend had lived his life. The message was this: At every crossroad in life, he had chosen to take the higher road. After all, it's the only one that leads to the top of the mountain."

We have the same choice. We can take the higher road and see what God has in store at the top of the mountain, or we can crawl abjectly on the lower road doing it our way.

21
Penguins

As we make choices in life, they often involve waiting. Surely, Emperor Penguins are an example of waiting. Huddled together for warmth in the frigid Antarctic winter weather, the male penguin sits on the egg for several weeks while the female heads to the sea for nourishment that she'll eventually regurgitate to feed her offspring. The male, meanwhile, battles snow, blizzard winds that can top 200 miles per hour, and icy temperatures that can dip to 60 below zero. The male takes the first watch, standing stalwart with his back to the freezing winds and the egg carefully balanced in a flap on the top of his feet. Never shirking his duty, he patiently waits for the return of the female penguin so that he can then head to the ocean for food. God has programmed penguins to be patient and to wait.[2]

While we don't necessarily think of ourselves as being programmed, as we walk in the Spirit, God can transform us so that godly responses become natural to us. The Scriptures promise that we can be confident He will complete the work He has begun in each of our lives. Philippians 1:6 says, *"For I am confident of this very thing, that He who began a good work in you will perfect it until the day of Christ Jesus."* Until the return of Jesus, we can expect that God will be molding, forming, shaping, transforming, and developing our inner person to be more like Christ. He wants to grow each of us in qualities such as patience, endurance, longsuffering, gentleness, and compassion. Only He can grow true spiritual fruit in us. We can't conjure it up by ourselves.

I'm reminded of a story our friend, Dave, told about a fruit tree. When the tree is getting ready to produce, you don't see it groaning, pushing, and striving to get a piece of fruit to appear on its branch. Fruit just appears naturally as a result of the limb being connected to the trunk which finds its source in the roots. It's the same with us. Fruit will naturally appear in our lives as we remain tapped into the Vine. John 15:5 says, *"I am the vine, you are the branches; he who abides in Me and I in him, he bears much fruit, for apart from Me you can do nothing."* If we are abiding in Christ, we **will** bear fruit. It will automatically happen. We don't have to struggle or try harder for it. It's simply a result of abiding. Then, when it appears, He gets all the glory.

If God's highest goal is for us to be conformed to the image of Christ, then why should we complain when perplexing or arduous circumstances come into our lives? If we believe that nothing comes into our lives without first being sifted through God's hands, then why are we distraught when experiencing uncomfortable situations? These were hard questions for me to contemplate. Perhaps this is true for you, too. This trial, and how I chose to respond, would reveal the reality of my faith and dependence on Him, and I didn't want to be found lacking. "Don't despise the things I allow to come into your life," became more than a catchy slogan for me.

Having traveled on the road marked "trial," I confess there were times I felt tremendous stress. Other times, I felt overwhelmed by it all. Sometimes I just cried. But underneath it all, I knew I was firmly rooted in the "Rock" of my salvation, and when I could walk no further, He would carry me. His presence was with me throughout.

Paul speaks about contentment in Philippians 4:11, *"Not that I speak from want; for I have learned to be content in whatever circumstances I am."* That verse expressed my goal. Notice Paul said that he "learned" contentment. That means it didn't come naturally to him. He didn't always walk into hard circumstances and immediately adjust. He was human and he, like us, wrestled as he went through the process. Even Jesus, "...learned obedience through the things He suffered." (Heb. 5:8)

His encouragement to us is that we can also come to the point where, no matter what comes into our lives, we will choose to rejoice and give thanks. We, like Paul, can learn to be content. The secret of Paul's contentment was that he trusted that God and God alone allowed situations to enter his life. He understood the authority and supremacy of Jesus, and he had given Him sovereign jurisdiction over his life. He understood the Lordship of Christ. He knew that God could be trusted to see him through anything life threw at him.

Key Principle #10 - Be aware of character qualities God is developing in you, especially attitudes and choices. There were things God wanted to teach me in the midst of this trial. It all had purpose. I trusted that God knew the best possible way for me to learn certain lessons in life. I knew that if I fell into grumbling and complaining about my circumstance, I would quench the Spirit and stall the things God wanted to build in me. The choice was mine to make.

22
Suffering

P aul endured much tribulation, yet he maintained an attitude of praise. He began his treatise in II Corinthians 11:23-28 by declaring his own unwavering faith in the midst of calamity. He pointed out that he looked like he must be insane. He had been beaten and imprisoned numerous times, five times lashed, three times beaten with rods, shipwrecked three times, stoned, in the midst of hunger, thirst, cold and exposure. We can read through that list and not be moved, or we can picture how we would feel in just one of those tragic situations. Paul had been promised that he would endure hardship in this life. The Lord went so far as to speak these words to him, *"For I will show him how much he must suffer for My name's sake"* (Acts 9:16). Knowing this was part of his lot in life didn't make it easier to endure, but it did clarify that he had a choice of attitude with each obstacle that came his way.

If I thought for one moment that things came into my life by chance, I would have been devastated as I dealt with Mother's Alzheimer's. God has boundaries around each of our lives, and He determines what can and cannot enter. Believing that brought me a measure of peace. God loves us too much to leave us to chance. He can bring good out of the most difficult situations.

John's Secret

In Revelation 1:9 John talked about being a *"…partaker in the tribulation and kingdom and perseverance which are in Jesus…."* I appreciate the three words John chose to describe his circumstances. Surely, John, the author of Revelation, understood tribulation as he lived during the time of Roman domination when Christians were threatened and persecuted, when emperor worship was promoted.

A word study reveals that tribulation can mean anguish, burden, or affliction, with a sense that suffering is a narrow or crowded experience. Perseverance is defined as patiently suffering, cheerful or happy endurance, with a sense of expectancy. Finally, between tribulation and perseverance is the word kingdom. This connotes a foundation of power and authority, of ruling and reigning. I think John understood a secret. The reason he could persevere in trials was because of the anticipation he enjoyed due to "kingdom" in his life. As he persevered in trials, his eyes were on the Kingdom of

God, the fountain of all that is good and right and just. His eyes were on Jesus, the author and perfecter of faith. He had discovered that this is the path to victory in any situation.

Ron

I'm reminded of our friend, Ron. He suffered for a number of years with terminal cancer and endured numerous chemo sessions. For anyone who has been in that situation, you know it's not fun. Yet, I will never forget Ron's glowing countenance when he expressed to us one day that he looked forward to each treatment. Mystified by this unusual perspective, we questioned him as to what he meant. He cheerfully responded that he saw each treatment as an opportunity to talk to people about Jesus. He said when he went in for chemo, there were nurses to talk to and other patients who were a captive audience. "I try to give them hope and I tell them that Jesus loves them and has a plan for their life." Up to his dying day, Ron was full of joy. He knew the secret that apart from Christ, life is truly futile and meaningless. God opened up ministry for him in the midst of the severity of his own very personal, excruciating trial.

Ron was an example of John's secret. When faced with his own personal affliction, he persevered with expectancy that God would bring good out of it. He leaned heavily on Jesus and kingdom principles, and he found God was faithful. Ron was a truly victorious man in the face of agonizing suffering. His life exuded the power and presence of the Holy Spirit. He was not caught up in works. He simply allowed Jesus to live through him as he rested in the Lord.

As we walk in the tribulations of life, why not look at them as adventures and holy callings that God has ordained for us? Although not experiencing the same type of pain that Ron suffered, this same outlook helped me to persevere and look to Jesus for victory.

The Bible teaches that, apart from Christ, life leads to futility. But did you know that futility for humankind is by design? It is part of the master plan of God. Romans 8:20-21 offers an interesting concept, *"For the creation was subjected to futility, not willingly, but because of Him who subjected it, in hope that the creation itself also will be set free from its slavery to corruption into the freedom of the glory of the children of God."* This speaks of the intentional futility of man apart from God.

God purposely created mankind so that we would eventually realize how pointless and hopeless our lives were without His grace, wisdom and strength. He did not create us to live life apart from Him in poverty of soul. It's His plan for us to live abundantly (Jn.10:10). God wants to set us free, and He is the only One who can. Even in the midst of something as devastating as Alzheimer's, God offered us hope in Himself, hope that He would always be there, that He would neither leave us nor forsake us, hope that He was unfolding a plan for our ultimate good.

A Guarantee

Often, character grows through uncomfortable situations in life, through suffering, or through choices we make. While the Bible promises that believers will prosper and have success as we meditate on the Word (Josh. 1:8), reaching that potential is usually dependent on our responses to various situations that come into our lives. My confidence grew knowing that nothing comes into my life without first being sifted through God's hands, including situations through which I must struggle. This proved a great comfort to me as I anticipated Mother's move to my town.

If the Bible guarantees anything, it is the certainty of suffering. While it was clear that Mother herself was suffering the ravages of a wasting disease, it was also clear that we who loved her were also going through a sort of fire. Those caring for an Alzheimer's victim, or for a person caught in any long term ailment, can understand. Alzheimer's is a heartless disease that literally eats the mind. Other diseases may destroy the body, but there is still a semblance of the person intact. With Alzheimer's, who the person is gradually disappears. Day by day, pieces of the mind are ransacked and plundered. The suffering of loved ones, who helplessly watch the process, can be enormous as well. Yet, with God, by faith it is possible to make the passage through with grace and consolation.

Several years ago, Bill and I went on an Alaskan cruise through the inside passage to Ketchikan, Sitka and Juneau. The inside passage is a waterway that goes up into Alaska, protected by land on both sides. We began our journey in Vancouver, BC with only a small part of the trip in the more volatile, open Pacific Ocean. Once on the inside passage, waters were smoother. I liken that to going through a trial with God. With Him, our passage through the trial is protected by "walls" on both sides; by His grace on one side and His comfort on the other. We do not have to go through trials alone. God desires to go through them with us. Isaiah 49:16 says, *"Behold, I have inscribed you on the palms of My hands; Your walls are continually before Me."* The storm goes on, but we are securely inscribed in the palms of His hands, known and protected by Him.

A friend shared with me that there was a practice among early Jews of putting marks on their hands by puncturing the skin with pictures of the temple. It reminded her of a tattoo. Their motive for these markings was to express the intensity of their passion and affection for the temple.[3] I found it warming to think of being securely inscribed on the Lord's hands in the midst of a trial. This verse told me that Jesus was forever aware, zealous for, and filled with affection for my mother and my family as we faced Alzheimer's together. We were all inscribed in the palms of His hands.

I Peter 4:12-13 makes an unusual appeal to be implemented in the midst of troubled times, an appeal to not be surprised by the trials life brings. *"Beloved, do not be surprised at the fiery ordeal among you, which comes upon you for your testing, as though some strange thing were happening to you; but to the degree that you share the sufferings of Christ, keep on rejoicing; so that also at the revelation of His glory, you may rejoice with exultation."*

What was happening to Mother and its effect on our family was definitely a "strange thing." But it was also an opportunity for all of us to share in the suffering of Christ, knowing there would be an eternal outcome. Sometimes, in the every day of life, it is hard to remember that we are on earth for just a few years. As believers, we will live with

God, face to face in eternity for thousands and thousands of years, actually forever. That perspective is difficult to grasp. Our minds can hardly take it in. We get caught up in the various trials of life here, and they tend to take over our thinking, even when we're exhorted in Scripture to consider trials as *"momentary light afflictions"* (II Cor. 4:17).

23
Count it all Joy

Our part in a trial is to rejoice. Now that's an amazing thought! How can we rejoice in the midst of a trial? James 1:2 even calls us to count it as joy when we encounter trials. In her study of the book of James, Beth Moore offered an interesting insight. She noted that in James 1:1, the simple and often passed over word "Greetings," in the Greek means "joy to you." With a play on words, James immediately proceeds in the next verse with *"Count it all joy my brethren when you encounter various trials."* On the one hand we are wished joy and on the other, it is our responsibility to accept, receive, and even embrace joy when we are in the midst of tests and tribulations. Beth explained that joy is part of our inheritance from God. It is our birthright. I find that concept comforting.[4]

What is the secret to rejoicing and counting suffering a joy? If suffering is to be a part of life, then God must have reasons why, and it must be important for our welfare. He must also have revealed a way to go through trials victoriously. While it is impossible to know all of God's reasoning, He has given some.

When suffering comes, it is an opportunity to be conformed to His death with a purpose of attaining resurrection. There is no resurrection without death. Clearly, some areas of our lives need to die. Some of our selfish or fleshly reactions need to be submitted to the Lord, so He can conform us to His likeness. Dying to self is so that God can raise us up to better serve others. While serving Mother, there were times I didn't want to be patient or loving. I didn't want to persevere and wait. It would have felt much better for the moment to have an outburst of anger or to back out of serving when I was busy with my own life. But God was in the process of helping me put off the old self and put on the new self.

Jesus died to self over and over. He made Himself available to the needs of others even when it inconvenienced Him. Much of His ministry occurred when someone interrupted His personal plans. He would be in need of rest, but people would call upon Him for healing, so he laid aside his plans. At times, he wanted to spend time alone or just with the disciples, but the requests of others beckoned. Jesus is all about people and meeting them where they are. Maybe, like Jesus, we need to consider interruptions as opportunities.

Servant-hood

Serving others is a calling for all believers and there is a wonderful picture of this principle in the Bible. In John 13:4 Jesus *"got up from supper and laid aside His garments; and taking a towel, He girded Himself."* Jesus, who had laid aside the cloak of His deity to suffer and die for our sins, humbled himself to become our servant. That's what "girding" Himself in the garment of a servant's towel stood for. Not only did he become a servant, but He became the lowliest of servants. Likewise, we have opportunities to lay aside our titles and positions, to humble ourselves, and be ready to serve those in need. Ephesians 2:10, *"For we are His workmanship, created in Christ Jesus for good works, which God prepared beforehand so that we would walk in them."* When we have a close relation with Alzheimer's, we have an opportunity to choose a servant's heart.

An interesting observation about being a servant is that Paul considered himself a bond-servant. He was a person who was free but made the decision to continue in the role of a slave. This was volitional serving. No one was forcing him. He wanted to do it. He recognized the call God had on his life and made a personal choice to put aside his own desires for the good of others. For Paul, this involved much suffering and persecution. Life was not comfortable. Paul certainly understood that trials were part of life, to be expected, when he wrote to the Thessalonians, *"so that no one would be disturbed by these afflictions; for you yourselves know that we have been destined for this. For indeed when we were with you, we kept telling you in advance that we were going to suffer affliction; and so it came to pass, as you know"* (I Thess. 3:3,4). Although not a similar situation, those caring for an Alzheimer's victim do suffer on a number of levels yet have the same choice as Paul...to continue in voluntary service.

Key Principle #11 - Accept suffering as part of life, and choose a heart of service. We either live selfishly or we live to serve God and others. Since Jesus came to serve, not to be served (Mk. 10:45), I knew I also had this choice to make. God wanted to make an exchange in my life. The process involved taking my self-centered heart and exchanging it for His heart of service in a new area. He would take my impatience and exchange it for His patience. He would take areas where I lacked mercy in exchange for His compassion. My part would be a willingness to consider myself dead to negative attitudes. His part was to then resurrect me, ready to be used for His purposes.

Bill offered a good visual explanation of the exchange we make with Christ. Suppose you have on your winter coat. When spring comes, you don't put your spring coat over your winter coat. You first take off the winter coat and exchange it for your spring coat. Then, when fall comes, you don't put your fall jacket over your spring jacket. You take off the spring jacket and exchange it for your fall coat. Without the exchange, we could have on multiple layers of coats. Likewise, the idea is that we put aside selfishness so that we can put on a heart of service to others. We put aside impatience so we can put on patience. We put aside harshness so we can put on compassion. The Christian life is an exchange of our selfish ways as we allow Christ in us to renew and fill us with His ways.

The Example of Joseph

Joseph is another example of this principle. You can read his story in Genesis 37-50. God made him successful, and he prospered in all that he did, but what were his life circumstances when the Bible said this of him? We tend to think of a prosperous person as one who does well financially, one who lives in comfort with all of his wants and needs met. That is not God's definition of prosperity.

When the Bible called Joseph successful, he had just been sold into bondage by his own brothers and lived in a foreign land as a slave. When it said he prospered in all that he did, Joseph was living in a dungeon. Unjustly accused of sexual assault by his master's wife, he served a two year jail sentence. That would probably not be my idea of prosperity, but in truth, his prosperity had little to do with happy, comfortable circumstances. It had everything to do with his attitude and response to his circumstances. The point is that we can prosper inwardly even when outward conditions look desolate.

Joseph could have been angry, bitter, and full of vengeance. He could have complained, grumbled, and screamed. Many would say he had a right to do just that. He could have howled, "This isn't fair! Get me out of here." Instead, he took the higher road and chose to see God's hand in the situation. Joseph knew the God He served. He knew that the only way to reach a mountain top was to take the higher road at every turn. God had given him promises which were yet to be fulfilled in his life. Just because Joseph was in a miserable, pathetic situation, he did not fold into a pity party. He chose not to whine, murmur, or harbor bitterness, but rather he forgave his brothers. God had given him a vision of his future through his dreams. It was enough for him to know that God was in control.

As a result, his righteous, mature behavior won him the favor of those over him. His godly response to his trials caused God to prosper him in whatever he did. Men meant evil towards him, but God meant it all for good (Gen. 50:20). Joseph grew in patience, endurance, and perseverance during his time as a slave. He understood tribulation, kingdom, and perseverance. God conformed Joseph to His own image, so that He would be put to the best possible service in His Kingdom, ultimately saving the nation of Israel. God made him successful because Joseph chose to cooperate with God's plan rather than to resist it.

God had to bring me to a similar point, clearly on a lesser scale than Joseph's monumental sufferings. Nevertheless, some changes were about to take place in my life, and I, too, had the choice of how I would respond. God had character qualities to build in me through His exchange program. Love, endurance, patience, and compassion for starters. I knew I wanted His will accomplished in my life, so I released my situation to God. By faith, I anticipated seeing His plans unfold as we moved Mother to Michigan.

Key Principle #12 - Cooperate with God's plan and consider seeing the situation as an "Adventure in God." Once we know God's intent in our lives, we need to flow with his plan. His plan may involve some struggles, but we can remember that God is working something good into our lives that will be profitable for us. I determined to look at Mother's coming to Michigan as an Adventure in God. Whatever this move brought, I decided I would consider it an opportunity to walk by faith, trusting that God had a plan, a purpose, and a way through each situation.

24
Adjustments

Although not excited about moving, Mother seemed to resign herself to the inevitable. Carl took her out for a farewell dinner Saturday night since we planned to leave Sunday. She shed no tears as they parted. I don't think she understood that he would no longer be part of her daily life. To her, it was just a casual, "Goodnight Carl, I'll see you tomorrow." He promised he would be there for the movers Monday, so off we flew to Michigan.

Upon arriving home, the first thing I did was phone Fay at the adult foster care home. As I had hoped, the room was still available. She wanted to meet Mother and seemed eager to have her as one of her boarders. I felt a flood of peace wash over me. I'm aware that not every family has the luxury of having a full time caretaker for their loved one. I was so thankful to have this provision for Mother. God had led us to this beautiful, warm home, and He had saved a place for Mother just when we needed it. Her room would be ready to occupy in one week. That meant she would stay in our home for seven days. As before, that week proved to be a full time job caring for her needs, helping her bathe, selecting her clothes, and generally keeping an eye on her all day long. And, of course, I listened to tales from her imaginary world as well. I was grateful that Bill jumped in and helped me as much as he could.

Both Mother and I had adjustments to make with each new change. One of the lessons I had to learn as she came home with us was that there were two roles I would be playing in her life, both equally challenging. While she was with us, until the foster care home was ready, I would be the loving daughter who would sit with her, love her, rub her back, sing to her, tell her stories, reminisce, read the Bible to her, and pat her hand. These were the soft things that she responded to, that made her feel loved.

The second role would be that of a caregiver, involving hour by hour assistance with every aspect of her life. That first week left me with a very clear understanding that doing both of those jobs was almost impossible. I gained a lot of respect and admiration for people who take elderly parents into their homes full time. The task can be overwhelming. I was shocked at how much work it was to care for another person's needs, especially an adult who had become somewhat like a small child. I was thankful that Mother would soon have a caretaker who would carry the day to day responsibilities, so that I could focus on being a daughter.

When I felt snowed under, I turned to the Scriptures and the Lord provided strength. He led me to Scriptures such as Matthew 11:28-30, *"Come to Me, all who are weary and heavy-laden, and I will give you rest. Take My yoke upon you and learn from Me, for I am gentle and humble in heart, and you will find rest for your souls. For My yoke is easy and My burden is light."*

This verse and others helped me to maintain a sense of peace, and to see that I could not do all that was required in my own strength. The weight of trying to live this adventure in my own power was impossible. When I put the burden of my worries and concerns on Christ, He carried them and my load was lightened. Bill suggested that when I tried to do things on my own, it was like a parable where a man loaded up his pack, placed it on the donkey's back, then proceeded to lift the donkey, carrying both the donkey and the burden. What a great picture. Why do we sometimes do just that?

Psalms 55:22 says, *"Cast your burden upon the Lord and He will sustain you; He will never allow the righteous to be shaken."*

Psalms 68:19 adds these words, *"Blessed be the Lord, who daily bears our burden, the God who is our salvation."*

Key Principle #13 - Lean on Jesus and His Word and allow the Holy Spirit to lead. Daily, I spent time with the Lord and often sought out Scripture that would strengthen and uplift me. Time in the Bible became especially important when I felt overwhelmed by the endless responsibilities I had. In those times, I needed to hear a word from God, revelation that would sustain me. There were times I stepped away from leaning on the Lord and tried carrying the load myself. I eventually learned that the load was lighter when the Lord carried the emotional weight of it. Slipping back in beside Him brought peace and strength.

25
Resistance

Overall, Mother's first week in Michigan went smoothly, until the day of her move. It was then that she announced, "I've decided I'm not going to move into that house, and besides that, I won't be staying with you any longer either. I think it's time for me to return home to Arizona."

In all honesty, I couldn't blame her. It must have been devastating to be moved around so many times against her will, to have other people take over even the most menial tasks in her life. From my perspective, these represented help and mercy, but surely, from her point of view, it felt demeaning. It was like a stripping process where we divested her of everything, including her will. In a sense, we considered her displays of will a healthy sign, though in the end she usually had to submit. Her feistiness showed she still had some life in her, still had some spirit. She had some ideas and opinions of her own, but even in times of trial, my mother remained a sweetheart and we loved her.

Mother became so insistent in her refusal to move that Bill had to have a gentle heart to heart talk with her one afternoon while I ran some errands. "Doris, we know this is a difficult move for you, but we have looked at all the options and feel that this home is the best place for you to live now."

"Well I don't have to live there. I'm going back to Arizona," she insisted with a downcast, somewhat defeated look in her eyes.

"Doris, the retirement home is no longer an option. They've said they can no longer provide proper care for you."

"I can get along fine on my own. I don't need any help," she snipped.

"Well, Doris, we have noticed that, although there are many things you can do for yourself, there are also things you now need help with such as laundry and bathing."

"I've always done those things for myself," she fired back.

Mother finally backed down a bit when Bill reminded her that others had been doing those things for her for the past year or so, since she hadn't been able to do them for herself. She soon quieted. Part of her must have intuitively sensed he was right.

"You have a choice to make, Doris. You can choose to fight, resist, be angry and bitter over the pending move, or you can choose to accept it, make the best of it, and go with the flow."

Mother seemed to ponder that and, for the moment, she acquiesced. I have always admired Bill's ability to say things that need to be said, but to do it with a fine balance of truth and love (Eph. 4:15). When issues have to be dealt with, even the most difficult ones, when addressed with a caring, sweet tone can prove to be palatable. Truth, when spoken softly and accompanied by love, is powerful and has calmed many a troubled soul.

Key Principle #14 - Give time for adjustment. Things changed in Mother's life at a faster pace now. Whether the change was large or small, she needed time to adjust, and we needed to be gentle and understanding of her emotions. Her mind had trouble assimilating even the simplest changes. To a degree, it soothed her when we took time to explain. How true that is for most people. When given a little time to think through decisions, words from a trusted friend can shed new light.

I was reminded of a verse in John 21:18, *"I tell you the truth, when you were younger you dressed yourself and went where you wanted; but when you are old you will stretch out your hands, and someone else will dress you and lead you where you do not want to go."* (NIV) This verse was so appropriate and surely represented Mother's life. She used to dress herself and walk wherever she wished. Now, she needed help with clothing and had to go where she did not wish to go.

Jesus, too, had to give up His life. His fate was in the Father's hands. Ultimately, His death glorified God. Perhaps watching a loved one deteriorate and lose independence could work as a reminder of the Savior and our need to follow and trust Him.

26
Moving Day #4

Mother had endured three moves in less than a year, and now her fourth was upon her. She had moved from her comfortable home to a retirement home. From there, she had moved into assisted living. Next, we moved her to our home for a week, and now she was going to an adult foster care home, albeit a truly lovely place to live.

Mother would have her own spacious bedroom and bathroom and, just down the hall, were the common living room, dining room, and kitchen, all furnished like a normal home. Her room was the closest to the living area, so she should have no problem finding her way around, or so I thought.

She seemed to adjust pretty well, although she asked about her furniture often. She was there a week before it was to arrive, and we were both looking forward to her being surrounded by some of her familiar things, especially her television. I hadn't revealed to her that much of her furniture would not be coming, that it simply wouldn't fit in the room. I had hoped she would have forgotten about it, just as she seemed to forget so many things, but the day the furniture arrived was an emotional occasion for Mother. Change is always hard for the elderly, but especially for those with dementia.

With agitation, she asserted, "Betsy, tell the movers to put my twin beds this direction in my room. And where will they put my couches?"

To anyone else, it would have been obvious that two beds plus couches would not have fit in her bedroom. Though her life had been reduced to bare necessities, her nesting instinct remained intact. She had plans for arranging her room, despite the fact that her mind failed to comprehend that an apartment full of furniture couldn't possibly fit into one bedroom. My heart sank as I watched her innocent, unknowing expression. I looked away as my own eyes clouded up. With great difficulty and a lump in my throat, I knew the moment of truth had come.

"Mother," I tentatively began, "I'm afraid we weren't able to move your beds. You'll be sleeping on the bed provided here."

I had originally hoped we could use Mother's bed, but when I looked over what Fay had in her home, I felt it was comfortable and would save moving Mother's bed. It had been sold at the auction.

"And your couches won't be coming either," I timidly added. I could feel my body tense as that piece of information settled in the air. I held my breath and watched her closely for the inevitable response. I'll never forget the pained, yet resigned look as her eyes pinched to hold back tears, and the color seemed to drain from her face. I so wanted to take her in my arms and tell her everything would be alright, that I hated having to make these kinds of decisions. I wanted to believe this was all just a bad dream, and when we awoke, her furniture would be there, and she could have it all. I wanted her to be happy, to be normal, to be my former mother, but she wasn't. So many things were different. I chalked up the event as one more time she had to relinquish her will to mine, although I'll admit I didn't like it any more than she did.

I visited Mother frequently the first couple weeks to help her with the adjustment. One night, I had a dinner engagement, so I took her with me. We returned about ten o'clock. As I began to drop her off just inside the door of her new home, she panicked. I was aware of her rapid breathing as her adrenaline kicked in. Confused and disoriented, she scanned the room.

"Where are you going?" she blurted out. "And where am I supposed to stay?" She was completely lost and had no idea where she was. Her home had become a maze of unrelated rooms with no apparent structure or way out. Taking her hand, I walked her through the living room and down the adjoining hall to her room, the first one to the left, a room she should be familiar with by now. We stood in her doorway as I reminded her that the bathroom was right across the hall. She had no recollection. Her mind was a fog. Perhaps the next day she would remember...or perhaps not. It must have been very frightening to not remember.

27
Where's Her Mother?

One afternoon, I stopped by for a visit to find Mother in a disturbed state, fidgeting and unsettled. As she paced around the room, she kept asking about her mother. "She said she'd be here, and I can't find her anywhere," agitation rising in her voice. She was clearly upset.

I listened for awhile and debated whether I should again tell her that her mother had died years ago. I'd done that before, and she usually just shook her head, but it stopped the turbulence in her soul. So, again with caution, I gently reminded her that her mother had died twenty years ago. This time, however, she looked at me with horror and painfully cried out, "Why didn't you tell me she died?"

Reminding her that she had been at the funeral was to no avail. Grief-stricken, she mournfully wailed, "This makes me feel like I don't even exist."

Mother was like a wounded animal trapped in a time warp. I began to realize the extent of her distress. It bordered on panic. I felt awful for bringing such anxiety into her life, even though her understanding was founded in unreality. We talked about other things in hopes that this moment would pass but, unlike others, it didn't. Then lowering her head she quietly murmured, "I don't think I can ever forgive you for not telling me my mother died."

For days I felt terrible, knowing I had made Mother so miserable. I began to wonder if, when she spoke of her mother, she was really talking about herself. It seemed odd that knowledge of her mother's death made her feel like she didn't exist. I remembered at times when she had been in our home, looking at her own picture taken several years before, commenting on it as though the picture were her mother. Regardless, I remembered that comfort was the goal, and it was best to avoid some issues. Haggling over something that would soon be forgotten seemed pointless.

I was a little wary when I visited Mother a few days later, expecting her to still be upset with me. I should have recognized that she probably would have forgotten the incident, most likely before I even left the last time. Happily, it had indeed been forgotten, never to be brought up again, certainly not by me. This vexing episode helped me understand that there was no need for me to carry a burden if Mother reacted to something I said. In this case, her memory loss was a good thing.

I had thought about apologizing for having caused her pain, but when I saw her again and she seemed composed and happy to see me, I felt that if I brought up the incident, she would probably have been puzzled and asked me, "What incident?" That day we had a sweet time together. Sometimes, her forgetfulness worked as a blessing. Facetiously, with tongue in cheek, I can't help but think of Paul's admonition in Philippians 3:13 *"...forgetting what lies behind and reaching forward to what lies ahead...."* Somehow, I don't think he necessarily related that to Alzheimer's, yet it was a good working principle at times with my mother.

Key Principle #15 - Change the subject when needed. Some subjects are quite disturbing for Alzheimer's victims. I had to become aware of which ones caused turmoil. When these subjects came up, I tried to change the course of the conversation to something more neutral. Often, the subjects that troubled her were irrational. Her mind would tell her things that were pure fiction. Believing them to be truth, she became upset. Changing the subject, instead of pursuing it, proved to safeguard her from much strife and unrest. At these times, her short term memory loss worked to an advantage. Usually, once the subject was changed, the difficult topic was forgotten.

I gave thanks that we still had many good times together characterized by lightheartedness, joking, and a general sense of contentment. We went for walks around her neighborhood on warm, sunny spring days, breathing in the fresh air and observing newly budding trees and flowers. We picked flowers from trees so she could smell them. Cupping one in her hand, she would carry it for the duration of the walk. When it began to crumble in her palm, she'd hand it to me to carry. I savored these sweet moments with Mother because I had no idea how long she would be lucid enough to enjoy them or to even recognize me.

Key Principle #16 - Savor sweet moments. Not knowing how long Mother would be with me, I made a conscious effort to watch for and savor sweet moments. I wanted some good memories of Mother's last years, not just memories of drudgery and fighting a disease. These moments became a valuable wellspring of peace and contentment for both of us in the midst of her struggles.

28
A Visit to the Doctor

After mother had lived in Michigan a few months, we made an appointment for a checkup to establish her with our family doctor. Dr. Brothers had been in practice for many years and reminded me of Dr. Welby, a favorite doctor on television in the 1970's. Like him, Dr. Brothers had wonderful bedside manner and would even make occasional house calls. He was deeply admired in the community. I would brag about him to my friends, that he was a master diagnostician. Any ailment anyone in our family suffered from, we could count on Dr. Brothers to identify, treat conservatively, and gain results.

On the day of our appointment, he took Mother's routine history, much of which I had to answer since she couldn't remember. He then began questioning her further as to her recall of abstract facts. It was quite apparent that she had trouble remembering anything. Dr. Brothers asked her to count backwards from one hundred by sevens. She confidently gave answers, but they were all wrong.

With a very professional tone he queried, "You seem to be having trouble with abstract thinking, Doris. Do you have any idea why?"

What a great question, but it was like a revelation to her. "Why, I have no idea!" she crisply spouted with astonishment.

As he continued his physical examination, Mother interrupted to announce, "You know I'm pregnant."

Without blinking an eye, Dr. Brothers calmly inquired in his usual relaxed manner, "When do you think you're due, Doris?"

"I'm not sure, but I've been pregnant for quite some time." Her lighthearted reply evidenced her obvious pleasure that he seemed to believe her.

With great reverence, he then proceeded to press his stethoscope to her abdomen, listening for a heartbeat. "Well, I don't hear any heartbeat. You must be in the very early stages. By the way, which pregnancy is this for you?"

"The second one," she answered without hesitation.

I thought Doctor Brothers was incredibly patient and kind to Mother. He listened to every answer, on the subject or off, with the greatest respect and esteem.

Mother had already announced her pregnancy to us when she lived in Arizona. I had not realized she would continue with that fantasy, but as she had gained a little weight, her clothes continued to fit more snugly than usual. Just for the record, I was

my mother's second pregnancy. She had experienced a miscar-
riage with her first pregnancy and lost a son. I'm not sure how
all this computed in Mother's brain. Cynthia was the second
live birth, so Mother could have been referring to her. But how
could we really make sense of any of it? It remained a mystery,
caught in the entanglements of Mother's mind. Logic, analysis,
and organized thinking were no longer reasonable expectations,
and any attempt to force them ended in frustration.

Key Principle #17 - **Listening is important**. Dr.
Brother's attitude toward Mother pointed out a significant
principle. He listened to every word she said, while affirming her dignity. He made no verbal judgments which would
have exasperated her. Rather, he chose to listen intently
with consideration to her feelings. His stance in this matter
confirmed to me the importance of listening with reverence
regardless of how irrational the conversation became.

Sadly, many years later, Dr. Brother's succumbed to
Alzheimer's himself. He was our neighbor, and it was sad watching the doctor, who had treated my mother with such grace and
kindness, become lost in the same world she had experienced.

29
Alzheimer's Seminar

With Mother getting settled and my life moving into a new and busier routine, I began to feel the need for some communication with others who faced the same kinds of issues with an Alzheimer's relative. As I prayed, once again, within a week or so, an article appeared in our daily newspaper announcing an all-day Alzheimer's seminar at a nearby nursing home. Discussion would focus on Alzheimer's disease and associated dementia. I immediately made plans to attend and felt God had answered another prayer.

The day of the seminar arrived and, as I entered the room I perused the sixty or so people who were caregivers, family, friends, or workers with elderly, dementia afflicted people. It warmed my soul to realize that I was not alone, that others also faced the same sort of adjustments I was facing. I enjoyed hearing the speakers, but even more, I relished input from the audience as they shared things they were experiencing on a daily basis. Some of the episodes they described were very amusing.

An attendant from a nursing home told the story of an elderly lady she cared for. Holding a brown spotted banana in her hand, the animated patient had insisted, "Do you see these brown spots? They're a secret code from the Russians. They're preparing to invade us. You must help me decode this message before it's too late!"

Being a rather reserved person, the attendant inspected the banana and replied, "Well I'm afraid this just looks like your ordinary banana to me."

The woman persisted that they must decode the spots, to which the attendant replied, "You are certainly creative."

Grinning, the woman countered with a twinkle in her eye, "Yes, and you aren't very imaginative, are you?"

A little humor is good for the soul and can lessen the tension of trying to interact with those afflicted with Alzheimer's. As long as it isn't cruel or dishonoring, humor can be a healing balm. Today, we laugh at some of the antics and things Mother said in her latter days. At the time they may not have appeared quite as amusing, but we always tell her stories with endearment toward the mother we honored and loved so dearly.

It's hard to know how far to go with some of the wild stories that Alzheimer's patients tell. The consensus of the group and the leader was to go along with the stories unless they brought harm to the person.

"After all," the speaker said, "Isn't that their reality?" Often, I wanted to bring Mother back to my reality, but her reality was what she knew at that time. She no longer felt comfortable in my reality. In fact, my reality no longer existed for her. It seemed to do no harm to let her dwell in her world, but I have to admit that something inside me still wanted to bring her back.

In dealing with Mother, I noticed that if I tried to bring her back to reality, it upset her and made her angry. The episode I had experienced where she couldn't remember her mother's death had been one such event. It seemed to create more emotional angst than going along with the absurdity and pampering her. Harmony usually prevailed when I chose to humor Mother, so that's the path I tried to follow in future conversations.

It's difficult to face the fact that this disease is progressive. I had trouble accepting that Mother was not going to get well. I prayed that God would mercifully take her home before the worst of the disease struck, before her brain deteriorated to the point that she no longer knew me. I hoped God would release her before her physical body also deteriorated due to scrambled brain signals. I travailed in prayer, wanting God's compassion on Mother, wanting her back to normal, wanting her liberated from the bondage of this disease, yet standing fully aware of the stark reality that Alzheimer's has no cure. In this life, she would not get better.

It was hard to imagine what Mother was thinking during this time. Since she did not speak of her condition, I could only go by signs that I saw as to whether she was suffering. Surely, she was distressed mentally during her times of agitation and frustration. I still wondered if she had any idea that her mind was no longer working properly. Or was she so confused that she didn't recognize that at all?

Bill's father, Lou, on the other hand, also endured Alzheimer's in his later years but was slightly different than my mother. While Mother rejected any thought of having dementia and therefore was unable to make plans on her own, Lou knew early on that something was wrong and correctly diagnosed his own ailment. We recall the phone call when he first told Bill that he was concerned about his mind, that he didn't feel he was thinking right.

Although knowledge of his state of being didn't help later on, it did add value to his early condition. Because our family understood that his mind was moving into dementia, with Bill's help, his parents were able to make early choices concerning what the next move would be for them. At first, of course, they hated the idea of having to move, but wisely they began to look for their next place to live. Together, they chose a very nice facility that was well set up with apartments, assisted living capability, an Alzheimer's unit, and a nursing home option, all of which Lou eventually used. The whole complex proved to be perfectly suited for their ultimate needs. When Lou later went into the Alzheimer's unit, Carmen, Bill's mom, remained in the apartment, but was still close to Lou. We were thankful, in their case, that it was possible for them to think ahead and make their own choices. How much harder it would have been for Bill's mom to have had do that all on her own. This way, Lou was at peace knowing he had made provision for his wife.

The original call Lou had made to Bill, where he expressed his concerns, must have been a humbling experience for him. For Lou, who had formerly been a very active executive and avid golfer, to forecast Alzheimer's in his life must have been extremely uncomfortable, if not alarming. Only a man who is incredibly strong can face that kind of fear and make a call like that. We were thankful to be able to help them make the decisions they needed to make. Lou, who had always been a devoted husband, would have done anything to make Carmen's life easier.

Dealing with Guilt

Something brought to my attention at the seminar was the matter of guilt. "It's common for family members of Alzheimer's victims to feel a sense of guilt that they're not doing enough," the speaker articulated. "No matter how much time we spend with a family member caught in dementia, a foggy sense of guilt can creep in and accuse us. The accusing voice has no rationale and comes regardless of the hours we dedicate to care-taking."

It helped to be aware of this insidious voice of accusation and to make a decision I could live with in caring for Mother. The speaker was right. Guilt feelings, alleging I wasn't doing enough or that there were other things I should be doing, did float across my mind from time to time. The amount of time to spend with her was an issue I needed to address. At first I went to see her every day to help her adjust to her new environment. However, I knew I couldn't continue to keep that schedule. I needed to find a balance between guilt and overload.

When Mother first moved near us, spending time with her seemed to swallow up my life. Before long, I realized I needed to decide how much time I could practically devote to her. What would be enough? As I considered my

192

long-standing priorities, I knew realistically that my own family had to come first and even take precedence over my mother, unless there was an emergency situation. If possible, I determined that Bill and Mike shouldn't have to suffer by a continually absent and harried wife and mother.

After discussing the matter with Bill, he felt it would be reasonable for me to spend time with Mother a couple times each week. I was so thankful for his counsel because it gave me permission to readjust to a more balanced schedule. I would not have to suffocate, nor would I have to feel I wasn't doing enough. Everyone has commitments and priorities, and it's easy to fall out of sync with needy situations that call out for attention. The plan we came up with gave me freedom. Unless Mother became ill, I tried to stay with it. Due to that decision and Bill's support, guilt rarely entered my mind, and the time I did spend with Mother was much richer and more treasured.

Bill stepped up to the plate and was a big help in visiting with Mother during each week as well. We both tried to make the most of our visits with her. Some call it quality time, we thought of it as comforting and reassuring time.

Key Principle #18 - Alleviate guilt by setting realistic priorities and choosing to live by them. Guilt comes when we think we're not doing enough. Once Bill and I determined realistic parameters of "enough," and I received Bill's help, guilt was alleviated. Blessed with a supportive husband, he would not allow me to become consumed with my mother. Several times, when I felt the desire to visit Mother every day, he said, "Resist the idea, Betsy." I appreciated his wise counsel. When Bill was asked by someone what role he was playing in all of this, without hesitation and with a twinkle in his eye, he replied, "My job is that of sanity." Bill was definitely a huge help in listening, and bringing perspective and balance to each situation that arose.

How easily we can become unbalanced by counting the urgent above the important. We all have lists of things that need to be done immediately. Unfortunately, they can be at the expense of the important things or people in our lives. I'm thankful for the support I had to keep my priorities straight while Mother was alive.

30
Odd Behavior

After a few months, I decided to write to some of Mother's lifelong friends around the country to let them know that she was now living in Michigan. I used her Christmas card list for this project. Since this was before computers were popular, many responded by mail, but one dear friend from North Carolina phoned Mother in her adult foster care home. What was odd was that in the middle of the conversation, Mother laid the phone on the table, left the room, and never returned. The friend later phoned me to ask what was going on. I explained the situation. She had not realized Mother had Alzheimer's. Later, I mentioned the call to Mother. She nonchalantly explained that she went back later to the phone, but her friend was gone, so she had hung up. We'll never know why she left the phone in the first place, and it apparently never occurred to her that what she did was odd. In fact, she was surprised her friend had not waited for her to return. I wonder how many hours went by before she did come back to the phone.

I was constantly amused, but at the same time stymied by some of the peculiar things Mother did, perhaps because she accepted her behavior as normal or at least without embarrassment. One day, I took her to our local hospital for a lab appointment for some blood tests. She walked up to the desk and told the nurse about how she used to have a live tiger sleeping on the bed next to her. People just don't know how to react to statements like that. We aren't geared for abnormal behavior.

Mixed feelings arose in me once again as she told her story to a perfect stranger. I wanted to explain why Mother said these kinds of things. I wanted people to understand this wasn't really her. It was a disease. A desire to protect her from humiliation welled up in my heart. Along with the compassion I felt for Mother, I had to admit that the stories she told were quite funny. I decided I might as well enjoy them for what they were. I certainly didn't want to dishonor Mother by correcting her in public, but often a smile or wink from me seemed to comfort strangers.

After the blood test, Mother went into the lady's room. She had mentioned several times that morning that her panty hose were falling off. With a quick peek, I had noticed they weren't on properly but were situated just above her knees. That would definitely feel uncomfortable and surely make walking an awkward experience. I supposed she was now in the restroom adjusting them. Ten minutes passed and I knocked on the door. She acknowledged my knock but didn't come out. Five more minutes passed, and it was now time for her X-ray appointment. Still, she didn't appear. Another five minutes went by and out she came, panty hose on one leg but not on the other, both shoes on, other panty hose leg a limp wad under her skirt. What a spectacle! Yet, so loveable....

In a hurry to get to the next appointment, there was no time to straighten the mess. As we arrived and sat down in the office, acting as if nothing was wrong, Mother casually mentioned that her hose felt like a puff-ball under her skirt. I then pointed out that she only had one leg in the hose and the other leg was naked. Except for the sensation of the balled up hose, she didn't seem especially bothered by her panty hose predicament.

"Would you like me to completely remove your hose?" I finally asked. With her affirmative answer, I proceeded to take off her shoes, pull off the pantyhose, which were now full of holes, and toss them in the nearby waste-basket. If you're thinking the people in the waiting room were surprised, what about the guy who eventually emptied the trash?

Key Principle #19 - Give your self permission to laugh.
Unusual as they were, I treasured these lighter moments as

a blessing and a way to keep perspective. Seeing humor in situations kept me in balance and provided much needed release. I tried to keep visits with Mother light hearted and fun, and we often joked with each other. Thankfully, she was still adept at thinking of witty things to say. On this occasion, I promised her I would diligently try to find a substitute type of support hose as soon as possible.

ॐ ॐ ॐ

31
Answered Prayer

The knowledge of the Lord's intimate involvement in every aspect of my relationship with my mother continually reassured my heart. One night soon after the hose incident, I awoke at 4:30 A.M. Wide awake, I began to seek the Lord. Emotional ups and downs, times of struggling followed by shafts of light, sometimes desperately needing to hear from God, all describe the state of my soul as I dealt with Mother's situation. This night I needed to hear from God. I was floundering.

"Lord, I need a word from you. I desperately need to hear your voice of comfort and encouragement tonight." I waited quietly for His voice. Soon, some words from Scripture floated into my mind. I felt instantly reassured that He was present. The strength and compassion of His words soothed my soul as I heard His familiar voice, *"I am the Lord Thy God, I Am."* It was a simple phrase, yet I had a sense of knowing that He was speaking to me personally. In the Old Testament, Moses asked God what he should call

Him before the people. His reply was, *"...Thus you shall say to the sons of Israel, 'I AM has sent me to you'"* (Ex. 3:14).

At that moment as I lay in the warmth of my bed, covers snugly tucked under my chin, I sensed a sweet calmness as God spoke to my heart. He reminded me that whatever my need, He was the *"I Am."* It was as though he whispered to me, w*hat do you need, Betsy? "I Am" the answer.* Caught up in the emotion of my mother's situation that night, I had not thought through just what I needed from God. So, I tried to clarify my thoughts. *What did I need?* After pondering for a moment, I knew what to ask. At the hospital, I had recently dealt with the episode with Mother's hose. I needed a source for a special kind of support hose that Mother needed for her varicose veins. The previous kind I had bought and disposed of at the hospital had not been what she normally wore in Arizona. Since we lived an hour from any mall, I had looked in catalogs and made some calls to various stores but could not find the right type of hose.

Several times in previous years, Mother had been hospitalized with phlebitis, blood clots in her legs. Because of that, it was necessary for her to wear heavy support hose at all times. Having support hose was not just something she wanted; it was a valid need for protection for her legs. As I sent up this simple request, immediately a thought came to mind that I knew was not my own. The thought was to go to our local Sears catalog store and ask for a Health Care catalog. Not aware that such a catalog existed, I felt confident that God was leading me.

The following morning would prove whether I had indeed heard God's voice. I slept peacefully that night, and the next morning after eating my usual bowl of Cheerios, I drove downtown to the Sears store. Stepping up to the desk, I asked the smiling clerk if they carried any kind of Health Care catalog. To my surprise, she cheerfully referred me to a nearby rack. "Right over there," she pointed. Pulling out the correct catalog, I quickly turned to the page with support hose. To my amazement, I found the exact kind Mother needed. I immediately placed the order, and she had them within days. Still today, I smile when I think of God's faithfulness, even in the small things of life. He is so extraordinary at providing all of our needs.

Sometimes it's the small things that cause the most anxiety in life. One time, a friend of ours told Bill that he only prayed for big issues, never for the small stuff. Bill questioned him about what kinds of things caused him to be anxious in life. As the friend began his list, it was apparent that it was all the small things. In truth, little issues tend to add up if not resolved. After some discussion, he saw the wisdom of bringing all things to God in prayer. Most of us have a few big concerns in our lives, but there are usually far more small things, irritants, habits of others, and inconveniences that bother us.

In John 1:38 Jesus asked His disciples, *"What do you seek?"* God had asked me the same question. *What did I seek? What did I need?* He promises to provide all our needs according to His riches (Phil. 4:19). He has a rich supply, an abundant, overflowing supply of anything we need. We serve a very practical God who delights in meeting the needs of His children. It's part of His very nature and character. He is the great *"I Am."*

I read a poem once by Helen Mallicoat that inspired me about Jesus as the "I Am." Perhaps you've heard it too. It goes like this:

> *I was regretting the past and fearing the future.*
> *Suddenly my Lord was speaking:*
> *"My Name is I Am."*
> *He paused. I waited. He continued, "When you live*
> *in the past with its mistakes and regrets, it is hard.*
> *I am not there.*
> *My name is not I Was.*

When you live in the future, with its problems and fears, it is hard.

I am not there.

My name is not I Will Be.

When you live in this moment, it is not hard.

I am here.

My name is I Am."

What else did I need? I needed peace, direction, and wisdom. I prayed and sought God, and as time passed, He met me at the point of every need.

32
Support Group

In the summer of 1990, I again felt the need to talk to other people who were coping with an Alzheimer's family member. At this time, no Alzheimer's support group existed in my town. With a deep and growing need for help, I decided to visit a group an hour away in the city of Kalamazoo.

There, I attended a meeting led by Shirley Heenan, a petite, vivacious lady who had lovingly cared for her Alzheimer's father until his death. The warmth in her eyes told me she was a woman of compassion.

As I settled into my seat, I observed there were about a dozen of us in attendance, a mixed group of men and women. All were dealing with a loved one afflicted with Alzheimer's. We sat in a friendly circle so as to see each other better and give everyone a feeling of inclusion. I was in rapt attention when the members of the group began sharing. While listening as they related their experiences, my eyes were opened to what seemed to me to be almost impossible dilemmas.

One lady related that her father, who lived with her, had stopped eating. After two weeks, she realized he needed care beyond what she could give. To her amazement, no facility in her community would agree to take him since he refused to eat. She ended up putting him in a nursing home in another town. Compassion and concern compelled her to make the forty-five minute drive each day to see him. Because of his wandering, the nursing home had elected to bind him in restraints all day, every day. He sat in one chair each day with his wrists and feet bound to the chair. His only release came during her afternoon visits when she took him for a walk. I felt so saddened by his situation. Seeing her once vibrant father humbled to the point of being forced into restraints must have been heartbreaking. It seemed so cruel, more like a prison sentence. I found myself riled at the thought of her father's ill treatment. My hope was that her circumstance was an isolated one. I choose to believe most facilities find alternative ways to handle such situations.

Her gratitude for the support group and the opportunity to share her situation touched all of us. It also gave her an opportunity to hear about the possibility of using organizations in her community who would visit her father several times a week. Shirley agreed to put her in touch with Hospice and other visiting health care professionals. My eyes were opened to an awareness of the many caring groups available to help people in this type of situation. In the end, we all felt more settled by these new possibilities. Sometimes, we just need outside information and perspective to solve a problem.

That evening, another group of three related people explained with distress that they all worked, so they had to move their mother with Alzheimer's back and forth between their homes. The situation had become a significant burden on all of them. Did anyone have a suggestion what to do with their mother? They felt it was no longer safe for her to remain at home alone all day. I understood why.

Because of the inherent forgetfulness involved in Alzheimer's, it is dangerous for them to be by themselves. They could start a fire, leave water running, wander outdoors in the cold and become lost for starters. I have heard of patients wandering off in the dead of winter without wearing a coat. Their ability to put together simple thoughts like putting on a coat or gloves may be gone. This family had too many complex issues to consider. Their situation was quite a burden. Happily for them, after some comforting discussion, Shirley helped them locate a suitable facility.

Many of us felt Shirley was a miracle worker. She seemed to have perfect answers to so many impossible sounding questions. I was touched by the stories I heard that night of people trying to cope. My heart went out to them. I realized afresh how God had truly undertaken for my mother by leading us to the home where she now resided.

Over the years, I have known people whose spouse with Alzheimer's eventually failed to recognize them. Some had become belligerent and hostile. One threatened to kill the caretaking spouse who feared for her life. One, no longer recognizing his spouse, asked for a divorce. Sometimes they tell the caretaker or spouse to leave. They don't want them there anymore. It can be both frightening and sad to face these quandaries with people who are so helplessly caught in the irrational mire of Alzheimer's disease.

In later years, my own father-in-law, Lou, in earlier stages of Alzheimer's, left their apartment one day and wandered off. Living in a retirement area of Arizona, Bill's mother frantically called the office. When a quick search did not locate him, they called the local police. Lou was later found two miles away from home, headed for their old townhouse. All that we can guess is that he remembered life as being better there. He was headed to what was familiar. Fortunately, it was not a cold day, but in Arizona, a hot day can be just as threatening.

33
Perspective

As I reflected on my mother's situation, I realized how much I had to be thankful for. Mother never became malicious or cantankerous. Yes, she was frustrated at times, but her sweet nature usually ruled. I was thankful she was being well cared for, and that we lived in the same town which made visiting easy. I thanked God for His abundant provision for her.

Realizing the plight of others in dealing with Alzheimer's, I took the opportunity to write a thank you note to Fay for all that she was doing for Mother. Her task of caretaking several elderly women must have been daunting at times. I know that more than once she had to wake up in the middle of the night to tend to Mother's needs.

I read an article, one of those email stories that travel the world, but I felt it was a wonderful description of the importance of perspective and giving thanks.

One day, the father of a very wealthy family sent his son on a trip to a different part of the country with the express purpose of showing him how poor people lived. He spent a couple of days and nights on the farm of what would be considered a very poor family.

Upon returning from their trip, the father asked his son, "How was the trip?"

"It was great, Dad."

"Did you see how poor people live?" the father asked.

"Oh yeah," said the son.

"So, tell me, what did you learn?"

The son answered, "I saw that we have one dog and they had four. We have a pool that reaches to the middle of our garden, and they have a creek that has no end. We have imported lanterns in our garden, and they have the stars at night. Our patio reaches to the front yard, and they have the whole horizon. We have a small piece of land to live on, and they have fields that go beyond our sight. We have servants who serve us, but they serve others. We buy our food, but they grow theirs. We have walls around our property for protection; they have friends to protect them."

The boy's father was speechless.

Then his son added, "Thanks Dad for showing me how poor we are."

Isn't perspective a wonderful thing? Makes you wonder what would happen if we all gave thanks for everything we have, instead of worrying about what we don't have.

Key Principle #20 - Take time to be thankful. I found that in the midst of troubling situations, no matter how bleak they appeared, there was always something for which to be thankful. Sometimes, I had to search for it, but I always found something. There was always someone in a worse situation. Hearing the heart wrenching stories told by the members of the support group helped me gain a fresh perspective for my own situation.

Hebrews 13:15 says, *"Through Him then, let us continually offer up a sacrifice of praise to God, that is, the fruit of lips that give thanks to His name."* It is good to know that God is pleased when we choose to offer Him thanks in the midst of a trial. There are times we may not feel thankful, when thanking God is more of a sacrifice. These are opportunities to thank Him by faith. By sight, we may not see anything for which to express gratitude, yet we know that God is always worthy of thanks and praise.

I hope you can join me in the following prayer. *Thank you, Lord, that you have a plan in this situation. Thank you, Lord, that I can trust you even when things look hopeless and desolate. Thank you, God, that Jesus is our provider and promises to supply all of our needs. Thank you that I am more than a conqueror, victorious, and triumphant because Your Word says that I am. Thank you for your love. Amen.*

Faith prayers of thanks can flow from our lips, prayers from our heart straight to God's heart. Some of my best prayers are when I use Bible verses and pray them. There are many prayers of thanks in the Scriptures. What could be more perfectly attuned to God's heart than a prayer from His Word? To pray Scripture is to pray God's perfect will. I'm convinced that at the heart of God's will is that we choose thankfulness.

34

When All Else Fails, There is Always Jesus.

God wants us to walk in faith regardless of circumstances, regardless of how despairing life looks, regardless of how impossible things seem. I'm reminded of a story my daughter Kim's pastor, Gregg Parris, shared during a service we attended in her Indiana church. He explained that there is a little known fact about Bobby Fisher, the renowned chess player. It seems that he had an interest in museums. Once as he walked through an art gallery, he came upon a picture entitled, "Checkmate." The painting depicted two chess players battling over a chessboard. On one side of the board sat a confident man with a little devil haloing his head. Gleefully, he pronounced "checkmate" to his bewildered partner who was portrayed as a man in a state of great angst with perspiration beading on his forehead.

Bobby pondered the painting for hours. He had a chessboard brought to him and set it up to duplicate the board in the painting. After reflecting and considering for some time, he rose from his chair and said he wished he could have had a word with the agitated man. He would have told him to let the devil have his move, that there was still one move left, and it would checkmate his opponent.

The pastor then compared this story to our Christian walk. When things look hopeless, when it looks like we're in a no win situation, when our best moves have left us ravaged and devastated, hold on because for a Christian there is always one more move and his name is Jesus. When the devil giddily commands his decree of "Checkmate," we can let him have his move because, in Christ, we always have the last move. Jesus will never fail us nor forsake us. We have much to be thankful for as we give the Lord praise for His many promises. They are sure, and we can firmly stand on their authority. So let's give a rousing, "Checkmate" to the devil. He will not overcome us. In the Lord, we can overcome. Even in death, for the believer, the enemy has not won. We read in I Corinthians 15:55, *"O death, where is your victory? O death, where is your sting?"* As believers, we know we have an eternal home waiting for us. That's why we can confidently stand on I John 5:13, *"These things I have written to you who believe in the name of the Son of God, so that you may **know** that you have eternal life."*

Our God is the God of the impossible. He says so in Matthew 19:26. I think He actually loves impossible situations. In fact, He majors in the impossible. When answers seem elusive from our viewpoint, that's when God loves to step in with a supernatural solution. We cannot outguess Him. He always has the upper hand. There were times as I dealt with Mother's situation when I was out of solutions. Dealing with some issues seemed to lead to a brick wall. But God.... He always had one more move, one I would never have thought of myself. I love the term, "But God." It's when we've come to a dead end, an impassable chasm. That's when God steps in and does something that changes the course of our world.

I'm reminded of the year 2004 when Bill had a stroke. When he started to communicate again, I realized he couldn't see. He was blind. Some days, I would enter his hospital room quietly.The nurse would have me stand in front of him, and she would say, "Look who's here, Bill." Bill would move his head around and not seeing me, would innocently ask who. My heart sank as I realized I might be taking a blind man home soon. He was unable to see me even inches away. I began to contemplate this new scenario and what it would look like on a daily basis. So many adjustments....

Almost immediately, something rose up in me, and I knew it was God nudging me to get people together to pray.

It seemed impossible that Bill could regain his sight, but I felt compelled to follow the nudging and called together a group of friends to pray. Later, they told me they had never seen me pray like that, with such boldness and confidence that God would restore Bill's sight. Together we stormed heaven for over an hour on Bill's behalf.

The next day, when I drove to the hospital to visit Bill, the first thing he said to me was, "I notice it's raining outside." Befuddled, I looked at him and asked how he knew that it was raining. Without hesitation he said, "Well, I looked out the window and saw it." Because he was heavily medicated in the hospital, I'm not sure he ever fully realized that he had been blind. From that day forward, his sight improved to almost normal. He still lacks lower left peripheral vision in both eyes but he's able to drive, read, and carry on a normal sighted life. In Bill's case, God had one more move. Checkmate!

35
A Visit from Carl

Mother's dear friend Carl moved from Arizona to Colorado as planned. He settled into a retirement home near his son and granddaughter. Though he was eighty years old, he remained alert and active. I'm sure he missed Mother as much as she missed him, maybe more so since he could better remember the sweet times they had together before Mother began to deteriorate mentally.

Carl still took road trips and one of them brought him through Michigan. He called us and made arrangements to see Mother. This would be such a wonderful treat for her. We both waited with great anticipation. It's good to have things to look forward to in life, and Mother had not lost her ability to anticipate some things, especially if it involved Carl. First, we counted the weeks till he arrived; then, we counted the days. Finally, the big day came. Mother had talked about Carl and wondered where he was on several occasions. Now, at the prospect of seeing him, she acted like a schoolgirl.

Fay had dressed her in a pretty peach cotton dress with a pastel floral belt. She had her hair and nails done at the beauty shop, and she looked radiant. Carl stopped by our house first and after greeting him, he followed me to Mother's home. Eagerly watching from the window, she rushed out to greet him, eyes dancing with hope and expectation. It was wonderful to see her so happy.

They went out to dinner at a local restaurant by themselves and returned to Fay's house early in the evening. Since Mother had always enjoyed her time with Carl, it had been a real boost for her to see him again. Carl later reported that not much conversation took place between them, but even so, I knew he met her emotional need for companionship that evening. I was so grateful that he had taken time to visit. I'm sure he was mindful of Mother's further decline, but always a gentleman, he treated her with the dignity she deserved. He was truly a dear friend.

36
Confirmation of Alzheimer's

As I observed Mother's continued decline, I decided it was time to again pursue confirmation of the disease from a doctor. In the early stages, she had a brain scan by a neurologist in Arizona, but at that time it was not conclusive. For my own understanding, I felt we needed another appointment with a neurologist, hopefully to confirm Alzheimer's this time. Although having that diagnosis wouldn't really change anything, I still wanted to know. There's a certain peace of mind when you know for sure what you're dealing with. A year had passed, and Mother had deteriorated considerably.

Since we lived in a small town, we didn't have a neurologist, but one traveled to our hospital from Kalamazoo for weekly appointments. We made arrangements to see him. On the day of the appointment, I handed him a list of Mother's symptoms which he found helpful. He then proceeded with his evaluation by asking Mother several questions.

"Doris, do you know where you are?"

"Why, of course!" she answered.

"Well where are you?" The doctor continued with a professional demeanor.

She looked around the hospital room and innocently, yet confidently, looked him square in the eyes and replied, "I'm in this building."

"How old are you?" queried the doctor.

"I'm in my 80's," was her prompt reply. (She was 76 but, interestingly, her mother had been in her 80's when she succumbed to dementia).

"What day is it today?" he asked.

"Why, it's Friday," she spoke with assurance. (It was Thursday).

"What month is it?" the doctor went on.

Pausing a moment, she pondered the question, trying hard to bring up the right answer. Looking around the windowless room, the best she could do was to say, "It's November." (It was August).

"And what year is it?" he asked.

Her face became pensive as she concentrated, determined to stir her mind to the correct response. "It's 19. . . 86," she replied with hesitation. (It was 1990).

"Do you know who the president of the United States is Doris?"

"Of course I do," she spurted, her eyes flashing as though her integrity was in question.

"It's. . . it's..." After a long, nervous pause, with eyes lowered, in hushed tones, she whispered, "I can't seem to think of his name right now." There was no way to compensate for this answer. Her lack of mental acuity was laid bare.

With each question, it grew more difficult for Mother to think clearly. My heart sank with her attempts to remember and to answer appropriately. She was trying so hard. Even knowing ahead that this was probably how the doctor's visit would go, I still felt a pang of sadness watching her valiant effort to save face and answer his questions.

Something we noticed over time with Mother, that is probably also true with most people with dementia, is that they attempt to answer questions in a way so as to protect themselves. They try to hide the fact that they don't really know the correct response. Often, the most loving comeback we can have is to simply let things go. The doctor, of course was not merely engaging Mother in conversation. However, in our situation we found it best to be careful not to ask questions that might be too difficult for her to answer but to simply move on if she showed hesitation. This is what grace is all about. It gave her a way to still communicate without the embarrassment of seeming ignorant. One thing we tried to avoid, but were sometimes unsuccessful at, was asking questions such as, "Do you know who I am?" or "Who is this, Doris?" Even for people who do not have dementia, it can be embarrassing not to remember someone's name. Who hasn't had that experience? In those moments, we sure don't want to be reminded of our forgetfulness, and we usually look for a gracious way out of the awkward situation. How much more humiliating for someone who truly can't remember, regardless of prodding.

The doctor pursued his evaluation further with more difficult questions, "Doris, as you've been watching television, I'm sure you've heard a lot about what's going on in Iraq. Can you tell me what the problem is over there?" Mother was completely baffled. She said that she had no idea. Unaware of the most important news headline for weeks, she was a total blank when it came to world events. I realized anew how much she had lost as I recalled our engaging and animated conversations about world events in earlier days.

Next, the doctor examined her ability to compute simple math problems. She answered correctly that there were four quarters in a dollar, but she also thought there were five nickels in a dollar, showing her thinking to be random at best.

Her confusion grew as he continued testing comprehension of basic instructions. When asked to touch her left ear with her right hand, she proceeded to touch the heel of her foot. Upon the doctor's careful repetition of the instructions several times, she finally did it right. But when asked to touch her right ear with her left hand and stick out her tongue at the same time, she was totally lost and found the task utterly impossible.

After finishing the last test, the doctor and I went out into the hall to talk. We left Mother to dress herself which, of course, she couldn't do. "Your mother is a classic text book case of Alzheimer's disease," he curtly explained. "There's no question about it."

I asked what stage he felt she was in. He explained that she was in the moderate to severe stage at this point then went on to say, "Since her symptoms have increased so rapidly in the past two years, you can expect continued rapid degeneration. I can't give you any hope or help. There would be no reason for her to visit with me further." He stated all this in such a matter of fact, rigid way that I was taken off guard. Case closed...door shut.

I rescued Mother as she walked out into the hall, underwear in place over her hospital gown. What a sight! Guiding her back into the examining room, I dressed her properly and left to face our tomorrows with the abrupt confirmation that

Mother indeed did have Alzheimer's disease and was in the latter stages.

37
Grief

I suppose this would have been devastating news if I hadn't already known her condition was Alzheimer's from my own observations, from the caregiver's observations, and from reading on the subject. For months, I had suspected that Mother had Alzheimer's disease. For me, reading ahead as to what was coming was helpful.

Though the news didn't shock me, the way it was delivered seemed so harsh, so final, so *this is the way it is. Now, go home and cope with it.* For several days following that office call, I felt listless and mildly depressed. Within time, I recognized these symptoms as grief. Throughout the disease, these times of grief came and went. Mother was dying in increments, and I was grieving in increments. Week by week, I was watching more of her mind degenerate, a curtain closing over the beautiful, classy mother I had known.

With the passing of each forgotten memory, I grieved. With the fading of each area of competency, I grieved. As abilities dismissed themselves from her life one by one, I grieved. I never knew when it would hit, but gradually I began to recognize that times of sadness were often times of grieving over further loss of my mother's capacity to function normally. I knew these abilities would never return.

Key Principle #21 - Allow time to grieve. Grieving is a natural, God given release for the pain and the sense of loss that we feel in life. I had not realized that a person could grieve while someone was still alive. It comforted me when I realized that what I was feeling had a name, and that name was grief. The feelings came and went and, although I didn't become engulfed or overwhelmed by them, I did allow them to run their course each time.

Elisabeth Kubler Ross and David Kessler have defined five stages of grief that people experience...denial, anger/guilt, bargaining, depression, and acceptance.[5] I found that of the five stages, many of them applied to me as I observed Mother's demise. Much of my mourning actually took place before she passed away. Everyone is different in their response to the sadness of losing someone. Some go through all five stages while others go through only some of them.

Denial to Acceptance

Cynthia and I had both denied that Mother had dementia at first. We found many reasons to excuse her behavior. Since both of us enjoyed good health, it was difficult to accept Mother's mortality or that she could have a mind related disease. We were sure she could still do things normally, and we reasoned that her behavior was to gain attention. We refused to believe her mind was troubled by a disease.

The frustration Cynthia and I felt was about the unconventional behavior Mother displayed. It was a concern that she was no longer acting with propriety. At that time, we were unaware that she was being propelled by something more sinister. When we agreed that I should bring Mother to Michigan, I realized that this decision automatically upped my care giving responsibilities with Cynthia only able to help on occasional visits. I know Cynthia suffered from wanting to do more, and I felt sad for her that she couldn't be there to help on a consistent basis. I appreciated her concern and truly had no hard feelings about the decision. Although we had agreed that this plan was best, she still longed to be more involved. We had discussed moving Mother to New York City where she lived, but it seemed impractical with

Cynthia's traveling work schedule. Besides, an appropriate residence there would have been much more expensive.

Some think that if they are the perfect caregiver, things will be okay again. This, of course, is not true and can lead to excess anxiety and frustration which are of no benefit. Cynthia and I faced the reality of the situation, once we educated ourselves about Alzheimer's disease, and learned to accept the road that we and Mother faced. We knew there were no medical answers, so there was nothing to bargain for in our situation.

Overwhelming frustration, sadness, loneliness, and abandonment can lead to depression. At times, I had mild depression, but recognizing its source helped me to gain perspective. Staying in touch with friends, and with the Lord, helped. I was blessed with a caring, supportive husband and three children who made themselves available to listen whenever I felt sad. Having people listen and empathize gave me the strength to go on.

As I accepted that Mother had Alzheimer's and that I was providing for her the best that I could, I came to a sense of peace. Commitment and love enabled me to continue helping her according to her needs. I also decided to accept Mother just the way she was and not to put pressure on her, or expect her, to be capable of doing any more than she could.

I acknowledged that she could no longer learn anything new and that her memory would continue to fail regarding many things she had once known.

This attitude gave me a sense of peace that I would not have had otherwise. I observed several situations where others expected Mother to be able to dress herself and perform simple tasks. When she couldn't, their frustration level rose. I also sensed frustration on the occasions when I forgot my decision to accept her the way she was, especially when I was in a hurry. Mother was never in a hurry.

38
Decline in Communication

Mother's communication skills soon declined noticeably. It became increasingly difficult for her to hold the thread of even a simple conversation. Earlier, her conversation had become bizarre and full of imaginations, but at least she appeared alert and responsive. Now, dialogue proved quite difficult. She often changed the subject in the middle of a conversation, and much of her chatter was irrational.

While riding in the car one afternoon she asked, "Is that a rabbit in the car in front of us?"

I pondered how to respond, wondering where this would lead. "You mean driving the car?"

"Yes," she said.

"Well, I think it's a man," I asserted.

"You'll have to take me to visit Betty today. I'd like that," she said changing the subject.

"That might be kind of hard," I carefully replied, "since she lives a thousand miles from here."

Her attention span on a subject seemed to be that of a preschooler. Conversation led nowhere, which was now typical. Often, she began a sentence and trailed off in the middle of it, her attention drawn to other things in her environment. I tried to bring her back, hoping to bring some continuity to her thinking, but she replied with nonsense.

Sometimes, she started a sentence and then, in the middle of it, she would pick up a magazine and begin reading aloud. In my opinion, this behavior increased because reading aloud seemed to center her on a topic and give her the focus she no longer had on her own. Perhaps, as she read the words, they formed something meaningful in her mind. Unlike her mind, the written words consisted of collected thoughts and seemed to give her a feeling of control. Unable to elicit concrete thoughts on her own, and no longer able to compensate, it's hard to imagine whether she could think much about anything, or if there was just a bunch of jumbled gibberish even in her thought life.

We had a conversation as we were sitting in her room one afternoon that gave me a picture of the reality of her entangled mind. As you will see, it was scattered and meaningless.

"Rail rats," she exclaimed.

"What do they look like?" I inquired.

"I saw one. They were real."

Immediately changing the conversation she said, "I heard Fay on the phone."

"What was she saying?" I asked, hoping it might shed some light on the rail rats topic.

By now, however, they were lost to her mind as she replied, "She said..."

Another pause and change in thought, "Did you bring anything that would be. . . ?"

"Oh." Looking at an envelope she now read the return address.

Opening a notebook on her side table, I noticed a life-saver stuck to the page. She often licked lifesavers, and we found them on everything from napkins to magazine pages.

"Oh, Dorothy," she began again.

"You mean the lady across the hall from you?" I queried.

"Yes, she decided to stop eating until...." Again the thought was lost. She turned her attention to a postcard from Cynthia and read, "I am in Ft. Myers."

Looking at me with animation, "Oh, you should have been here this afternoon. You should have been here."

Back to the postcard, "Dear Mother, I am in Ft. Myers."

"What happened this afternoon?" I asked with peaked interest as I tried to nudge her mind back to a topic.

"Well, this lady had decided some time ago she was not going to eat anymore and so…"

Back to the postcard.

"What happened when she decided not to eat?" I pursued.

"Nothing, I was just surprised he came to the door and I invited him in."

"Who?" I asked.

"I went to the door."

"Who was there?" I again asked.

"That was… Dear Mother, I am in Ft. Myers."

Clearly her thinking had degenerated to a befuddled state. Nothing made any sense. Frequently, her memory for the names of people and things failed. Sometimes, she hesitated in a sentence. Occasionally, I gave her the word. At other times, she described the word and asked me for it. Most often, I let her search for a word that would fit in the sentence. I felt her integrity was at stake and wanted her to feel she could do it without my help, if possible. There were so many areas where she had to have assistance. I was running out of ways to help her compensate.

I've wondered about some aspects of her mental abilities. It was interesting that, while she grasped for words and her memory often failed her, she still remembered how to read. Perhaps that would indicate there are different levels of memory in the mind. It's like not remembering something, and then you stop thinking about it, and suddenly it pops into your mind. In the same way, it's possible to turn off your mind, yet read aloud. Our eyes go over a page, recognizing words and how to pronounce them, all the time thinking of something unrelated. It is possible to read words with no comprehension or memory of what we've read. We've all done that.

Just when things moved into a murky haze, a hint of lucidity would come forth from Mother's muddled mind. A refreshing bit of humor would dispel her intellectual fog like a shaft of light. Such an occasion occurred as we drove along a side street one afternoon. Mother noticed a number of birds gathering on a lawn.

"Look at all those birds," she exclaimed. As we passed by the street sign, she observed it said "Hatch Street." Turning her head to read the sign, she commented, "I guess that's why there are so many birds!" Well, it took some processing to come up with that comment. I felt both amused and encouraged that day.

Besides dwindling in ability to verbally communicate, I began to notice a waning in her listening capabilities as well. She misheard a number of words. One example took place at the doctor's office when he had told her to touch her ear. She had heard the word "heel," when the doctor clearly said "ear."

This mix-up of words was the cause of much strange communication until the real word entered her mind, if it ever did.

Deterioration of communication became more obvious as I called to mind how acute Mother's memory was before Alzheimer's. I remembered the many animated discussions she and I had enjoyed over the years. How alert and informed she used to be. Always a very sharp, intelligent woman, Mother was well read and could discuss any current event or issue. She had always been an avid reader of all kinds of material, and we had many lengthy discussions concerning politics, religion, and social issues. In retrospect, there had indeed been a great decline in her ability to converse with intelligence. She had no idea who held the office of president, what day it was, or even where she was. Truly, she had become like a helpless toddler, without the knowledge or wisdom to make any decisions on her own.

Research on Communication Decline

Something I love to do is research, thus I have explored many subjects that intrigue me. Occasionally, I have sought out diagnoses for medical issues concerning me or a family member. I like word studies in the Bible, and I have done a lot of Ancestry research for both my family and Bill's. So, it was normal for me to "hit the books" regarding Alzheimer's. My findings were interesting.

As I researched the degeneration of communication skills in Alzheimer's, I found a very helpful section in the book, "When Your Loved One Has Alzheimer's," by David L Carroll. He explained that in the first stage of Alzheimer's, there are delays in responses. Because victims often can't think of the proper word to use in a sentence, they will try to describe it. For instance, if Mother couldn't think of the word comb, she might say, "that thing that gets the knots out of my hair."

Typically, if a person can't think of words, he might change the topic. In the early stages, it might be embarrassing when words can't be recalled. Most of us have had the occasion when we couldn't remember a word. We tend to joke about it. In Alzheimer's, the frequency of this deficit increases dramatically.

In the second stage, conversation ebbs as mistakes increase and more words are forgotten. Because extra effort is required to find substitute words, the victim may abruptly change the topic, never returning to the original subject; or he may withdraw from verbal interaction altogether. Sometimes, not understanding, he asks for things to be repeated. It may appear he has a hearing problem, but it's his logic that is deteriorating, not his hearing. He is no longer grasping the meaning of conversation. Following even simple directions falters in this stage.

In the third stage, there is an increase in the inability to find the word he wants as vocabulary further diminishes. Conversation, if at all, seems scattered and nonsensical.

Finally, in the fourth stage, difficulty in communicating becomes severe. He is unable to understand even of the simplest concepts and is incapable of communicating with any meaning at all.[6]

It helped me to have this kind of resource to understand what Mother experienced in communication, to know what to expect next and how I might handle it graciously. Though literature on Alzheimer's was meager in those days, I was thankful for enough to stay somewhat informed and updated.

39
Missing Rings

Mother seemed to settle into the routine of the adult foster care home as well as could be expected at this stage of her disease. The other ladies being attended to in the home seemed very congenial. Even though conversation was sparse between them, it was comforting for her to have others around.

Mother's symptoms, however, continued to multiply on a weekly basis. Concerned one day, when I noticed her diamond ring was not on her finger, I asked where she had put it. She had no idea. We looked in the obvious places in her room, under the bed, on the bed, on her table. It wasn't there. I later found it in a bathroom drawer in my home. She had apparently hidden it there on one of her visits.

With hesitation, I decided to give it back to her, all the time wondering where I might find it next. She still had a ring on the other hand that she hadn't lost or misplaced. Wanting to be optimistic, I thought perhaps this episode was a one time event. Within a week, however, that ring also went missing. I later found it under her bed. Next time I visited, I noticed both rings were missing. When I found one of them in her jewelry box, I decided it was time for me to remove it to a safe place in my home. I was pretty sure she wouldn't miss it. Fay later found the other ring, which I quietly took as well. Mother had always loved jewelry, so I had mixed feelings about removing her rings to a safe place. She later questioned where they were, but thankfully, soon forgot all about them.

Trouble Dressing

Mother entered a difficult stage in her illness soon after moving to her new residence. Her last effort toward independence descended with a rush of assertiveness. Although, unable to perform the daily tasks of dressing and undressing, she adamantly refused to allow Fay to help. She resisted every effort made to assist her, yet she could not do these things for herself. It became a daily frustration for Fay.

Unyielding and insistent that she do it herself, Mother made Fay's job of dressing her tedious, sometimes taking hours to complete. The culmination of many weeks of obstinate resistance came when Mother struck Fay. Totally out of character, I was shocked to hear she had actually hit her caretaker. What could possibly have prompted this kind of behavior? There had to be a reason. Rational or irrational, I had to understand what motivated my mother to this action, so unlike her character. She had never physically harmed anyone in her life.

As we visited one day, I decided to see if I could get to the bottom of her clash and abuse toward Fay. "Mother, Fay tells me that you hit her the other day. Is that true?" I asked.

"Yes," she coyly answered.

"Why would you do that?" I queried.

"She steals my clothes," she promptly replied with intolerance in her voice.

"Why would she steal your clothes?" I was incredulous.

Swiftly, her rationale came to light. Mother didn't want Fay to touch her clothes because when she undressed her, Mother observed Fay taking her clothes out of the room to be laundered. Unable to grasp the logic of that concept and without the forethought to ask, she had concluded that Fay was stealing her clothes when she saw them leaving the room.

"Mother," I explained, "when Fay removes your clothes from the room, it's to wash them. Then she brings them back clean."

I'm not sure whether she gained full understanding of that idea, but her behavior ultimately changed. Apparently, this explanation satisfied her and, as time went on, Fay reported she became easier to care for after that.

40
Another Support Group Meeting

The next month, I attended another Alzheimer's support group. This one had recently formed in my town. Again, it was good to have a place to share with and listen to people who really understood what life was like with Mother. Similar to the last meeting I had attended in Kalamazoo, this one also helped me gain further perspective as I again heard from people whose situations were puzzling. We all appreciated understanding that we were not alone.

One distraught lady lamented about her Alzheimer's husband. They had been married for about fifteen years, a second marriage. He had been an engineer and a wonderful husband. Now with Alzheimer's, he didn't recognize her and repeatedly asked her who she was and what she was doing in his house. This, coupled with his continual reference to his first wife, left her deeply hurt. When she asked him who he thought she was, he replied, "I haven't the faintest idea, but you sure are a good housekeeper!"

Another lady warmed our hearts as she spoke of her mother who had Alzheimer's. She expressed that she considered it a joy and a privilege to serve her mom as long as she could. Her mother lived with her family because she felt she couldn't be alone. I was impressed with this woman's devotion, her willingness to serve, in essence to lay down her life for her mother.

In view of the self centered, "me first" society we live in, I found her attitude refreshing. While many people seem to find sick, elderly people a burden and a nuisance, she had chosen to walk in the Biblical principle of counting others as more important than self. I applauded her stance.

A Holy Calling

As I considered her approach and the deterioration process of Alzheimer's disease, a meaningful thought entered my mind. Although Alzheimer's is a devastating disease, God had allowed me to care for my mother during this sad time in her life. I felt, in a sense that He had entrusted my mother into my hands. Ultimately, for this season of my life, I was responsible for whatever went on in her life.

I felt humbled and honored that God had chosen me to perform such a task. In the book of Esther, chapter 4:14, it says, *". . . and who knoweth whither thou art come to the kingdom for such a time as this?"* (KJV) I knew it was not an accident that I was there for my mother. Perhaps I was born "for such a time as this."

Key Principle #22 - Consider care taking a holy calling from God. I believe God ordained my care taking responsibilities toward my mother, and I regarded them as a holy calling that He had on my life. This thought helped keep me in perspective. God had made me a steward of her life. Paul says in Ephesians 3:2, *"if indeed you have heard of the stewardship of God's grace which was given to me for you."* Like Paul, God had given me stewardship of His grace to bestow on my mother. A steward is someone who manages something that belongs to another person. My mother belonged to God. My task was to pour out His kindness, mercy, love, and grace upon her. It was an awesome assignment and surely a holy calling.

Colossians 3:23-24 says, *"Whatever you do, do your work heartily, as for the Lord rather than for men; knowing that from the Lord you will receive the reward of the inheritance. It is the Lord Christ whom you serve."* From these verses, I concluded that when I served my mother, I really served Christ. Therefore, the love of God compelled me to do my work heartily. It was the Lord whom I served.

"For I know the plans that I have for you, declares the Lord, plans for welfare and not for calamity to give you a future and a hope" (Jer. 29:11). Although God entrusted me with a stewardship of grace, mercy and compassion towards Mother, this verse indicated that God also had plans for my life through this situation. It would indeed be possible to prosper through this difficult trial. There was nothing I could do to bring Mother back from the abyss of Alzheimer's, but I began to realize afresh that God is sovereign in all things. According to His perfect plan, He had charted me on a course too, one which He had personally designed and mapped out to fit my life and His purpose for it.

Looking back on the opportunity I had to love and serve my Mother through her illness, I can see many things the Lord produced in me. I am overwhelmed at the fruit of this experience, the character, love, and heart that God developed in me during what I thought, on many days, was pure drudgery.

While I was contemplating the admirable attitude the lady in the support group demonstrated, I noted an elderly couple sitting across the room. The man and his wife remained quiet throughout the meeting, listening to all that we said about our various Alzheimer's relatives. Many symptoms and problems were discussed and much help expressed. Finally, the man spoke up and revealed to the group that his wife, sitting next to him, had recently been diagnosed with Alzheimer's disease herself. A respectful, or perhaps, stunned hush fell over the group. I think we were all hoping we hadn't said anything that might have upset her. All of our eyes rested on this petite, shy looking woman. Her sad, yet empty eyes, thin face, and wispy hair, somehow reminded us of our own relative in the early stages. Gradually, we all viewed her in a new way. We felt admiration that she had come to this meeting, yet sorrow as we contemplated the road ahead of her and also what her husband would be dealing with in the future.

It was eye opening for many of us to hear her testimony. She was very aware that she showed the early symptoms of the disease... memory loss, trouble with communication and bringing words to mind. She looked about sixty years old, young for Alzheimer's, yet she remained fairly cognizant. I wondered what thoughts went through her mind as she heard us share about the more advanced stages of the disease. And how was her husband processing our discussion? They both faced a long road ahead. While I know they were enlightened that night, I hoped they found some encouragement as well.

Key Principle #23 - Find a support group. Joining a support group helped me to stay in perspective. It also provided a place where I could share with people who could empathize because they were in a similar situation. They understood. Many of the members had suggestions that had worked for them. We bonded over our shared plight and savored the opportunity to encourage each other simply through listening.

41
Further Mental Deterioration

As the weeks went on, Fay noticed Mother's increased mental deterioration. I had to agree that I also observed this. One afternoon I took Mother for an outing. As we left, she tried to go out by way of a closet door. She had lived in this home for a number of months but was still stymied by where things were. Steering her gently, I guided her away from the closet and out the front door.

When we returned later and walked through the living room toward her bedroom, she commented, "Why, I don't believe I've been in this part of the house before." In truth, she had been through that part of the house on her way to every meal.

Getting lost in the house was a common occurrence. Forgetting where the bathroom was, she often lost her way. It was still just across the hall from her room, of course, where it had always been. After Fay led her out of her room and into the bathroom, Mother frequently forgot why she was there, and Fay had to remind her.

The downward spiral of Alzheimer's was beginning to affect Mother in new areas of forgetfulness. Until this point, Alzheimer's had only taken its toll on her mental faculties. If that weren't devastating enough, now the disease began to deteriorate her physically as well. I knew from reading that this would eventually occur, but each new stage was still a shock requiring further adjustment. The human brain is such an amazing organ, able to guide the activities of a myriad of bodily functions. Gradually, Mother's brain forgot to send signals, or the signals became garbled on the way to fulfill their role in her body.

Due to this change, it became difficult to take her out. When she first came to Michigan, I had allowed her to choose a church to attend. She chose one not far from her home that had a service similar to the kind she was accustomed to. A kind couple had volunteered to pick her up each week for the Sunday service which was such a big help. Now, with Mother's incontinence, it became too much of a burden, no longer a safe or practical option.

So, I began taking her with us to the Sunday evening service at our church, knowing I could help her with any indiscretions. She enjoyed the praise and worship music, joined in the clapping, and kept rhythm by tapping her fingers on the pew in front of her. Inhibitions melted away as she joyfully raised her hands in praise to God, something that was not usual in her church experience. She smiled throughout the service and enjoyed catching the eye of any babies in the congregation. Mother thrived on the fellowship, and happily, she quickly felt at home.

Being a social person, she loved being around people, and I tried to offer her occasions to socialize to the degree she was able. However, taking her to the grocery store sometimes posed a problem. Where she used to approach strangers on our outings and engage them with her unusual stories, she now insisted that she knew the people she stopped in the store. Baffled, they graciously explained that they were sorry, but they didn't recognize her. Several times, I had to guide Mother on down the aisle and distract her with my grocery list, so others could continue their shopping.

On several occasions, as we neared the cash register, I had to return items she had put in the cart when I wasn't looking. I usually tried to catch her pulling things off shelves so we could put them back at once, but some things missed my eye.

Mother's need for socialization, coupled with her irregular behavior, sometimes led to frustration for other people. In the adult foster care home, she wandered from room to room getting into the possessions of the other ladies when they were out. Not only did she get into their things, she also took some of them and hid them in her room. Once, I found five items that didn't belong to her. Of course, she had no idea who they belonged to or how they had arrived in her room.

I had to chuckle one day when the mail arrived. Mother had been called for jury duty in Arizona. For a fleeting moment, I contemplated putting her on a plane and allowing her to perform her civic duty (only kidding). But I did find some humor in thinking of her on a jury in her present state. That would have been some trial!

Fall came and with it Thanksgiving soon arrived. We had the whole family in our home for a traditional festive dinner. Mother joined us, but the day left her agitated and shaky. All the commotion, so many children running here and there disturbed her and tested her emotions. She stood in the hallway at one point, crying as she looked at a picture of herself. "Why are you crying, Mother?" I sympathized.

"I'm upset because I don't think I did enough for my mother," she explained. Mother had become a child in so many ways. I had to support and encourage her as though she were a vulnerable young girl. Although saddened and tormented by what seemed so real to her, I was glad I could be there to help her navigate through her maze of beleaguered thoughts.

A highlight of her week came when she went to the beauty shop to have her hair set and her nails painted. Fay and I considered it important to help her look as good as possible. She always appeared so fresh and pretty after her trip to the beauty parlor, and I'm sure it was good for her soul to be doted on. Who doesn't love a little pampering?

The time came, however, when I realized I would have to do her nails for her. After having them freshly painted at the shop one day, without thinking, she laid her hands in her lap. Her best suit skirt received a large smear of polish, and her nails were ruined. I don't think she ever realized what she had done. I sent the suit to the cleaners and, fortunately, the polish came out, but from then on, I did her nails at my home. After painting them, I would lay her hands out flat on paper towels, compliment her on how pretty they looked, and remind her countless times not to move her fingers and ruin her newly painted nails. I hooked up the hair dryer and blew them dry before she moved and stained anything, all the while coaching her to keep her hands still. This procedure worked well and enabled her to continue to have the polished nails she had always enjoyed. One more area of her dignity maintained. One more opportunity to honor her.

42
Kathryn

One of the blessings God provided for me during this time was the opportunity to become acquainted with some of the other ladies in the adult foster care home. Five ladies now lived in the home along with Mother. Two shared a room and the rest had their own room. Near the back door entrance, where we usually entered the house, was Kathryn's room. Hooked up to an oxygen tank twenty four hours a day, Kathryn spent much of her time in bed. Seeing people come and go past her door provided her meager socialization. At best, her existence was tedious, often accompanied by labored breathing.

Since I passed by her room on every visit to Mother's room, Kathryn and I often greeted each other and chatted a bit. She occupied herself with television, reading, and a rare guest. Telling visitors about the latest old movie she had watched helped her pass the time. I couldn't help but think how wearisome and monotonous her life had become in her latter years.

As I prayed one morning in my home, a thought dropped into my mind that I immediately recognized as coming from the Lord, *Why don't you tell Kathryn about Me?* Each time I prayed after that, the same thought recurred.

Give me the opportunity and I will, I promised the Lord.

In a hurry one day, I dashed over to see Mother and stopped for a quick hello to Kathryn. She began to tell me about her life as a younger woman. Progressing quickly through her life to her present bleak situation, she ended with a statement that jarred me. "I wish I would just die," she lamented. "Living has become so difficult." I know now that there are many elderly people who share this same sentiment, but that was my first time to hear such painful words.

Realizing this was God's open door, I carefully moved the conversation to the Lord. I asked Kathryn if she knew for sure that she would go to heaven when she died. "I don't know," she sighed, eyes downcast with a look of despair. "I hope so but I don't think I'm good enough."

I shared some of God's plan, but feeling rushed, I asked if I could come another day and share some Bible verses with her. Smiling, she said she'd be pleased to have me come back.

Several weeks passed and I thought of Kathryn often. On the occasions I thought I might visit with her, she either had company or her door was closed, meaning she was asleep.

Still, I began to sense an urgency to go back and talk with her more. I almost sensed the Lord planned to keep her alive just long enough for her to resolve some important spiritual issues in her life.

Finally, the opportunity presented itself and we moved right to conversation of the heart. "Kathryn, I've been thinking about the last time we visited and how you said you didn't think you were good enough to go to heaven. I want you to know that I have some good news for you. Your access to heaven is not dependent on how good or bad you've been. God has a different and better plan to offer. Would you like to hear about it?"

Eagerly, she affirmed that she definitely would like to hear, so I read aloud Billy Graham's pamphlet, "Steps to Peace with God." It's a wonderful, short explanation of the salvation plan. It speaks of God's love for each of us and how He has a wonderful plan for our lives. Because of sin, however, we are separated from God. But God, in His plan for the redemption of mankind, sent Jesus to pay for our sin by dying on the cross. His resurrection is proof that who He claimed to be was true. Our part is to accept His finished work on the cross and to receive Him into our heart. Salvation is not dependent on what we do but on whom Christ is and what He did for us.

"Have you ever accepted Jesus as your personal Lord and Savior, Kathryn?"

"Yes, many years ago," she answered with a far away look, "but I've never read the Bible. Please read more of the pamphlet to me," she pleaded.

Recalling her earlier comments about lack of assurance of salvation, I read I John 5:11-13, *"And the testimony is this, that God has given us eternal life, and this life is in His Son. He who has the Son has the life; he who does not have the Son of God does not have the life. These things I have written to you who believe in the name of the Son of God, so that you may know that you have eternal life."* I explained to Kathryn that, from these verses, she could know that she would go to heaven. We prayed together, and I noticed that a peaceful glow warmed her face as she thanked me and we said good-bye.

I saw Kathryn briefly on one more occasion. She again expressed her appreciation and thanked me profusely for sharing the pamphlet with her. "I've read it over and over," she exclaimed. "The Bible verses have meant so much to me."

Kathryn went to be with the Lord the next week. I was grateful that God had given me the opportunity to share His love with her before she went home to meet Him. It was heart warming to know that I could be used as His messenger wherever I happened to be, and that God was eager to give me opportunities to speak into the lives of others.

43
Christmas Season

Christmas of 1990 arrived with its usual bluster of cold, wind, and snow. Amidst all the preparations of baking, shopping, and wrapping presents, we looked forward to family coming and celebrating together. However, Mother spent Christmas week in the hospital with the flu. At first, I felt sad that she had to be in the hospital on Christmas day, but soon I realized that she had no awareness that it was the holiday season. My explanations of the time of year were consistently met with a distant gaze, void of comprehension. I might as well have been speaking in a foreign language. To her, it was just another day on the calendar. Although sad, this knowledge made the season tolerable, knowing that she wasn't pining away in a hospital bed wishing she could be with family. Still, we missed her presence during this festive season of celebration.

Our daughters, Kim and Laurie, were visiting, so I took them to see Mother one evening. We sang her some Christmas carols and set up a small Christmas arrangement I had purchased in hopes of bringing some cheer to her hospital room. I sensed that Mother had no idea why I brought it. She smiled and enjoyed the time with us but continued to seem oblivious to the reality of the holiday.

We had lots of company in our home through the holidays. Besides our children and their families, we entertained friends, and my sister and niece from New York. Busyness further escalated with added frequent visits to see Mother in the hospital. Although the nurses and doctors were attentive to her needs, there seemed to be a barrier in their understanding that Mother could no longer communicate properly or with intelligence. Everyone acted as though she was normal and as though they believed everything she said. The staff asked her questions and regardless of how she responded, they treated her answers as correct. I also couldn't depend on Mother to accurately report to me what the doctor said each day. That was now beyond her capabilities.

This became especially frustrating when I discovered the nurses were giving her two medications that she hadn't taken for months. In her misguided state, Mother had affirmed their use. It made me wonder what else I was missing. Because of the seriousness of issues like this, I began to time my hospital visits according to when the doctor would arrive so that I could speak to him personally every day.

Through this experience, I realized the importance of someone being an advocate for Alzheimer's patients. They truly need someone to walk through their illnesses with them. They are incapable of making decisions or even looking after their own self interests. I was glad I could do this for Mother but felt sad because many patients didn't have anyone who had the time or ability to be there that often. I shuddered at the consequences Mother might have endured if I hadn't caught just the medication issue in time.

Besides Bill's wise input and perspective, I became Mother's only advocate in decision making concerning her care, what tests she should undergo, and how to proceed in her treatment. The responsibility weighed heavily on me since I couldn't move into the hospital but felt I needed to be there frequently to be proactive in advocating for her.

As I had done so often with others, again I whispered to the doctors, nurses, and attendants, "She has Alzheimer's." They seemed to recognize what that meant, yet they assumed that she could still communicate normally. Some of them began to speak louder which forced me to explain that her hearing was fine.

"Doris, have you been taking your pills?" they bellowed. I'm sure I have, on occasion, done the same thing with elderly people. It almost seems like a natural response to raise your voice when around them. I think Alzheimer's was such a new diagnosis in the medical field that even healthcare workers were still unaware of exactly what was involved with this disease and how to respond to it.

Since her hospitalization only involved complications from the flu, Mother returned to Fay's home after a week. Fay worked laboriously to strengthen her and help her to walk again after being in bed for so long. Wisely, Fay realized that if Mother stopped walking for very long, she might never walk again. Already compromised, her brain could lose its memory of how the process of walking worked. It is a fight that the elderly battle in general...simply to stay on their feet. Although not a victim of Alzheimer's, Bill's mother fought vigorously to maintain her ability to walk. She even had both knees replaced at the age of ninety. With the help of a walker, she was successful, though in constant pain for the last five years of her life. Too late, we realized her operation had not been performed correctly.

During Mother's recuperation, she and I had some sweet visits. I read to her from a new Bible Kim had given her. We prayed together, and I tried to build her up spiritually while Fay helped her regain physical strength. Often, I read articles from Guideposts magazine as she listened intently to the accounts of people who had overcome difficulties in their lives. I hoped in some way the stories would comfort and strengthen her. One thing that I felt convinced of was that not all communication is through our ears. When I read from the Bible, I was confident she heard in her spirit. Altogether, we laughed and had warm moments of intimacy as she recovered from her hospital stay.

A Window of Lucidity

On one visit, Mother sat in her rocking chair gazing into space. A window of clarity surfaced as she remarked for the first time, "I don't know what's wrong."

"What do you mean, Mother?"

"I can't seem to finish my sentences," she replied.

For the first time, I had an opportunity to quietly take her hand and explain to her that she had a disease that had taken away her ability to think clearly. I asked her if she noticed that she had trouble remembering things. When she said yes, I gave her just enough details about the disease to calm her soul. Most likely, this conversation was quickly lost from her memory, but I was so thankful for this opportunity after many months of wondering if she had a clue as to what was going on with her mind. It would be the only time she ever brought it up. I felt better knowing I, at least, had a fleeting moment to talk to Mother about her ailment.

Mother's strength returned in part, but her illness had taken a permanent toll physically. One blessing on the heels of this illness was that her agitation and wandering passed. She seemed more tranquil and spent most of her days sitting in her chair or resting in bed. No more pacing, wandering into other people's rooms, or removing their belongings.

Television became more of a companion, but her mind caused her to think she took part in the programs. She frequently told me she had attended a ball game or a symphony. Often she mentioned visitors she had. At first I was puzzled because I couldn't imagine who would be stopping by to see her. I soon realized they were characters from a television show she had seen. Still, I was thankful that she had a television to help pass the long hours of each day. Mercifully, it seemed that Alzheimer's victims had a different awareness of time than most people. It didn't seem to bother Mother to just sit all day, whereas it would have driven me crazy.

❧✦❧

44

A Visit to Our Home

When Mother recuperated enough to go out, I brought her to our home for a meal. While visiting, I showed her some mail that had arrived. I had learned earlier that mail sent to her residence either remained unopened, or she hid it. On more than one occasion, I found sealed envelopes in an obscure location. I wanted to make sure she had the opportunity to read her mail if it was from a friend. If any business mail arrived, I needed to be aware of it as well, since I was now the one responsible for that aspect of her life. Mother could no longer be accountable for paying bills, answering calls, or sorting mail.

She still loved receiving cards, however, and read each one over and over. They seemed to momentarily connect her with the real world and remind her of the warmth of friendship. One dear friend, Dolores, faithfully wrote every week. She had been the in home caretaker Mother had hired when my father was bed ridden with cancer. Over time, she and Mother had become dear friends. Although Mother was unable to

263

fully comprehend the cards she received, they were calming for her and encouraged both of us greatly. Words expressing her appreciation for Delores' continued outreach went unspoken, yet Mother enjoyed reading the cards multiple times.

Once, I tried to encourage Mother to respond to another friend by writing a thank you note. I brought her a pretty card with a floral motif and pointed out where she should start writing. With much prompting, she wrote a short note, although I observed she had forgotten how to form many letters, and her ability to spell had diminished substantially. I don't think I sent it. After that, I decided to write the notes myself. Most of the time, however, Mother wasn't able to carry through a thought long enough for me to write a complete sentence.

During her visit, we perused a family album together. When I showed her a photo of Kim's husband, she had no idea who it was. More and more, people vanished from her memory, although at this point, she still seemed to recognize me. On another occasion, she failed to recognize our son, Mike, and called him Philip. There's no way to know where she came up with that name, but at least she was trying.

By now, I had learned that Mother needed to be closely monitored when she came for a visit. Of course, the lady in our bathroom mirror still disturbed her. With an accusing voice, she ruminated how unhappy it made her to see "that girl" in our home. Bill had spoken with her about it in the past and again gently asked, "Doris, you know who that is, don't you?"

"Well, yes I do," she answered in a sheepish way that told us she recognized herself. We were hopeful for any sign that she was back in reality. But it was not to be. With the next breath she acted as though "that girl" was her enemy again. She lived in parallel worlds, where her mind was a relentless prison from which she would never truly escape.

During her visit, Mother sat down in the living room and looked at the magazine section of the newspaper. She spent time talking to pictures of Tom Sellick and Burt Reynolds who appeared on the front cover. Soon, I called everyone to gather at the table for dinner. As we sat down, Mother surprised me with an admonishment for being a bad hostess.

"What do you mean, Mother?"

"Why, you didn't even invite my friends to dinner!" Her reprimand took me aback.

Baffled, I asked, "What friends are you talking about?"

"Well, Tom and Burt, of course!" Her answer rang with an annoyed tone. In her mind they were her close friends.

I recalled how upset she had been in the retirement home when others at her table had not acknowledged the magazine pictures she had brought with her for dinner. Thinking how I could appease the moment, I mustered my confidence, entered her fantasy world, and replied in the most gracious way I could. "Oh Mother, I did ask them, but they said they had already eaten." The exchange reminded me of when I used to play dolls with Laurie. The only difference was that Laurie knew we were pretending. In any case, my answer settled Mother down and we all enjoyed our dinner. This was one more example of going along with, rather than challenging, her truth. I entered her world, played along, and came up with an explanation that made sense to her and certainly put her at ease.

Later, as we got in the car and headed back to Fay's, I fastened her seat belt and made sure nothing remained on the seat between us. Mother frequently picked up anything left on the seat and took it with her, regardless of what it was. She inadvertently picked up things in our home as well. I'm still missing some of my recipe cards, although I found two of them in one of her purses at a later date.

Alarming Symptoms

Just as Mother gained back strength from her Christmas hospital stay, she had what appeared to be a TIA (Transient Ischemic Attack), also known as a mini stroke. She began babbling, had trouble walking, and was generally weak. Her head also listed to the right. Later, X-rays showed no sign of a stroke, so we weren't sure what this episode was, although it repeated itself several times in coming months.

Awakening one morning with terrible chest pain, Fay summoned an ambulance to take Mother to the hospital emergency room. It turned out to be a digestive problem. They treated her and sent her home. Since Mother was like a small child in so many ways, unable to communicate what was wrong, we all tended to overreact at times.

About this time, Fay left on a long overdue vacation, leaving a lady named Stacy in charge. I had already become acquainted with Stacy who was frequently in the home to help and had already bonded with Mother. She was clearly worried when Mother required a hospital stay. When Mother returned, Stacy generously decided to set her alarm for every two hours at night to get up and check on her, making sure she received the best of care. I thought that was such a compassionate, selfless gesture from Stacy. She had other ladies to tend as well, yet she set aside her own sleep to be sure Mother was comfortable during the night shift. I pray God will bless Stacy, wherever she is today, for her kindness to my mother.

With Mother's continued demise, I began to consider the intrinsic worth and value of every human life. So little remained of what she could do for herself. Even the most basic human functions had to be done with the aid of others. Yet, she was created by God and He had a purpose for her life. Sometimes, I laid awake at night concerned about her, yet I knew that her life remained highly valuable even in face of her continual deterioration.

45
Trudy

I visited Mother more than usual after her hospital bouts. Trudy, another lady in the adult foster care home, lived across the hall and down a door from Mother. She suffered from senile dementia. One afternoon, I arrived for a visit around lunch time. Fay had set a bowl containing a canned peach half at each ladies place. I couldn't help but watch as Trudy tried to cut hers up. With each attempt, the peach circled around the bowl like it was playing "catch the peach" with her. At last, I volunteered to cut it up for her and successfully fed her a bite. Then, handing her the spoon, she also managed to retrieve a piece, but on the way to her mouth, it fell to the floor. Offering her a paper towel to clean up the juice that had landed on her sweater, I then wiped up the floor. Glancing up, I found Trudy eating the paper towel. What more can I say….

Mother and Trudy, without conversation, had somehow bonded. They "hung around" together. Often, they were the only two left at the table after a meal; Mother folding a napkin over and over, reading any words written on it, Trudy just sitting and dozing. They found a certain comfort in each other's presence. No words needed to be exchanged, each one was just there. The unspoken, yet understood, need for companionship exists even in those suffering with dementia.

Trudy regularly wandered into Mother's room. Agitated and usually mistaking me for someone else, she frequently apologized for things she imagined she had done to offend me. Not once did I have any idea what she was talking about, yet her need to feel placated led me to soothe her with reassuring words.

I liked Trudy. Her demeanor exuded a "woe is me" attitude, yet with a little provocation, she could quickly place a warm smile on her face. With her head hanging low and her composure disconcerted, she pleaded, "I wish you would just make me disappear. Can you make me disappear?"

Her voice usually sounded like a slow, drawn out moan. She reminded me of Winnie the Pooh's friend Eeyore, always sad and moping about something. When asked how she felt, Trudy answered with a quivering sigh, "Oh, I guess I'm all right."

Once, I took her along with Mother for a walk around the block. Holding both of their hands, we slowly made our way down the sunny street. "Trudy, this is the day the Lord has made. We should rejoice and be glad in it," I joyfully spoke. "Trudy, look at all the beauty of God's creation around you. Are you rejoicing today?" I lightly teased, hoping to cheer her.

"Oh, I guess I am," she mournfully groaned, her pouting eyes glancing up for attention. Attention I could give her, but it was never enough to bring her out of her slump. I wondered if that had been her demeanor throughout life or if she had been more vibrant as a younger person, more hopeful, more outside of herself. Questions I will never have an answer to, but knowing Trudy helped me to make some decisions about my own life, helped me to rethink how I come across to people. What attitudes do I carry? What better choices could I make?

Another Hospital Stay

As our walk with Trudy continued, Mother began to feel weak about half way around the block. I hoped we could make it back to her home. Periodically, we stopped and rested by standing in place for a few minutes, then continued on. I really couldn't leave Mother to get help, and this was before the era of cell phones. So, we had to continue making progress toward our destination. We were only half a block away from their home, but it seemed to take eons to get there. Arriving back, Mother felt winded and was glad to sit down and rest.

As the day wore on, she didn't seem to bounce back. All week she remained fragile. I began to feel more than a little concerned about her condition. For the first time, I began to consider that Mother might die soon. I tried to emotionally prepare myself for that eventuality. My emotions went up and down like a see-saw. Would she die soon or live for many years? Bill prayed with me, and I tried to release my apprehension to the Lord. The future seemed to contain many unknown factors.

When her condition did not stabilize, I wondered if she should be in the hospital again or if she should at least see the doctor. One minute I thought I should call for medical help, the next minute I wasn't sure. I didn't want to be calling for every little thing. I've never been one to rush to the doctor but I did feel turmoil mounting in my soul. *Lord, send me someone with words of comfort and direction,* I prayed.

Mother, in her weakened state, experienced mid back pain, garbled speech, and her head listed to the right again. She had difficulty walking, felt sleepy, and had a hollow look in her eyes. She had been in the hospital once before with the same symptoms, but they had eventually dissipated on their own. The decision to see a doctor again seemed questionable. Her symptoms concerned me, but what more could they do for her? Back and forth, I vacillated.

I had no sooner breathed a prayer of desperation, and the phone rang. A friend, who was also a nurse, called to see how Mother was doing. God used Anna Mae to console my fears and concerns and suggested I check in with the doctor. With that affirmation, my prayer was answered. No more waffling. Interestingly, the minute I ended that call, the phone rang again. Mother's doctor was calling to say he wanted to see her right away because something appeared unusual on an X-ray she had a few weeks prior. So I helped Mother dress, carefully guided her to the car, and off we went to the doctor's office.

46
Hospital Confusion

One look and the doctor immediately arranged for Mother to check into the hospital. Another episode that looked like a TIA. I drove her to the emergency room, helped her into a wheel chair, and wheeled her up to the admitting desk. Having laid awake much of the night concerned about Mother, I was exhausted. The receptionist at the desk, busy on her computer, looked up at me over her half rimmed glasses, as if to say, *Who are you?* Without thinking I offered, "I'm her mother." Realizing immediately what I had said, with a tilt of my head and a bemused look, I finished with, "Correction, I'm her daughter. I just feel like I'm her mother." We exchanged an amused smile. Mother missed the banter as she nodded off for a quick snooze. I had to chuckle. But the truth is, in elderly years, it is often the children who have to take responsibility for parents when they are no longer able to care for themselves. It's a sad, yet honoring position to have to take over.

Again, as with her last stay in the hospital, I had to inter-vene on Mother's behalf. The physician's assistant soon realized Mother's answers couldn't be trusted when she volunteered the year was 1917. Other staff members were harder to convince and continued to ask her for answers she was incapable of giving. They actually believed some of her "off the wall" answers. I suppose Alzheimer's was still new enough that some in the medical field didn't comprehend the scope of the brain's collapse with this disease.

I continued to whisper, "She has Alzheimer's," although I sensed there was no longer a need to protect Mother from hearing. She was past the reactionary stage.

In the hospital, Mother soon rallied. Our daughter, Laurie, and her husband Brian, arrived for a visit. "Mother," I asked, "Do you know who these people are?" (I know... I've already said that's not a good question to ask anyone. However, at that time I hadn't yet thought that through).

"Well, of course I do," she answered with a giggle.

"Well, who are they?"

She studied them for a moment, trying to remem-ber, trying to save face and avoid embarrassment. "That's Warren," she said with conviction.

"You mean, Brian?" I appealed. Her vacant eyes told me that she had no idea who they were. She seemed to

275

recognize their faces but couldn't connect them with names. So, I introduced her. "This is Laurie, remember? She's your granddaughter." Then I told her about all her grandchildren and her great granddaughter, Erika. Mother listened intently while playing with a string on the bedspread. I'm quite sure she had no idea what I was talking about.

We had a pleasant visit. When her dinner arrived, I helped feed her. The last time I had offered to assist feeding her, the bed ended up covered with salad. This time, I brought along a bib, which I neatly tied around her neck in hopes of a better outcome. I proceeded to carefully aim each bite. Despite my best attempts, food still landed everywhere. What a disaster! In the future, I requested help from the staff, leaving meals to the professionals. I would spend my time just being the daughter.

We thought Mother had suffered another mini stroke, but a CAT scan only showed the normal brain atrophy that accompanies Alzheimer's disease. In the latter stages of Alzheimer's, doctors have noted that the immune system also weakens. People don't die from Alzheimer's. They usually die from other complications, often involving infection such as pneumonia. It's even been said that pneumonia is the old person's friend.

As difficult as Alzheimer's was to cope with, I felt it was easier to accept than the physical problems that manifested in the latter stages of the disease. They ranged from bowel problems to pleurisy to bladder problems, among others. Top that off with her inability to communicate about her ailments, and it was often very stressful. It became more difficult to get her attention, and her interest in any conversation waned. My stress level rose because of this, and I would lay awake at night thinking and praying about her physical problems and discomfort. Watching the physical decline was painful.

Something to Ponder

Another elderly lady roomed with Mother in the hospital. I overheard her male relative mournfully whispering under his breath as he left one day, "I can't stand this anymore." I began to think how healthy people are often repelled by sickly, elderly people. There exists in our midst a quiet world of people struggling in the shadows of life. Most of us rarely have contact with them, but they exist just the same. We seldom see them unless we purposely visit a hospital ward, a nursing home, or as in my case, an adult foster care home.

Some of us are suddenly thrust into this world when we, or someone close to us, enters it. Otherwise, we live life almost oblivious to its existence. Why are we sometimes disturbed by this world? Is it cultural or just human? Is it the strangeness of watching as a human being deteriorates? Is it that their condition brings us an awareness of our own mortality? Are we afraid of our emotional reaction? Truly, it requires a sense of mercy and compassion to feel comfortable in the presence of those afflicted with serious ailments. I asked myself these searching questions.

I was reminded of Bill's mother, Carmen. She had lived many years in Michigan where Bill's dad had worked. They had been a very popular couple in the community. Later, like my parents, they had retired to Arizona, but Carmen eventually moved back to Michigan to be near us when she was close to ninety. Her husband was gone and she felt the need to be near family. This time, however, she rarely had a visitor other than family. It was sad.

But then a bright spot came for her when a friend of ours, Loretta, asked if she could visit Carmen and get to know her. They spent many happy afternoons together. Loretta took her on several outings and began to speak to her about the Lord. Bill's parents had always resisted conversation about our beliefs, but something began to stir in Carmen.

One afternoon as Loretta was about to leave, Carmen asked, "Well, aren't you going to pray with me?"

Puzzled, Loretta asked what she would like prayer for. Carmen, surprised that Loretta didn't know, responded with "Aren't you going to pray with me to receive Jesus?" This was the moment Loretta had hoped, prayed, and patiently waited for. Actually, our whole family had prayed for this moment for years. On that sunny afternoon in an assisted living home in Michigan, Carmen Tacchella invited Jesus to be her Lord and Savior. As the Bible affirms, the angels in heaven were rejoicing that day. And we later joined in with them.

A speaker once said, "How we treat an Alzheimer's patient, or any frail elderly person, depends on our view of the worth of a human being." There are prominent people in our society who say people with Alzheimer's are of no value. Some philosophically say that an Alzheimer's victim is dead because he is no longer capable of worthwhile activity. As Christians, we proclaim the intrinsic worth of every human being. As long as a person remains alive on this earth, he deserves the best possible care and attention. Our family wholeheartedly agreed with this viewpoint.

Faith Dispels Fear

Living in close connection to a relative with Alzheimer's made me acutely aware of the symptoms of the disease. I was close to fifty at the time and began to wonder if I personally showed any signs. I'm sure most people who have a family member suffering from this disease contemplate whether they also will be a victim. I heard of one young man who had several Alzheimer's relatives. He said that knowing this had caused him to give up on life. What was the point of marrying or having his own family if eventually he would succumb to this terrible disease? From my perspective, that was a hopelessly sad way to live.

I feel blessed that I don't share his sentiments. They sound so bleak. As a Christian, I am not a person without hope. Although I have occasionally pondered whether I will ever have Alzheimer's disease, I know with assurance that I have a God who orders the steps of my life. God has plans for each day of my life, and I have chosen to expectantly live them for His glory. Today my mind is fine. I will live this day for Jesus. I can't worry about something that might or might not happen. What a waste that would be. I only have now, and I choose to be productive this day.

Alzheimer's is an enemy I cannot control, so I have chosen to trust God with my future, and I have found that faith dispels fear. What possible good could come from tormenting myself today about a future possibility? While I choose not to dwell on possibilities, I do remember God has promised that believers will be transformed and given a new, whole body at death. I am comforted to know that was true for my mother as well. God wins when it's all said and done.

47
Alzheimer's Seminar

I n March of 1991, I attended a "state of the art," daylong Alzheimer's seminar put on by the Michigan Alzheimer's Association. I found it tremendously helpful and affirming. Having accepted my mother's condition for what it was, I wanted to stay well informed about the disease. This seminar met my need for the latest information available. Many of my questions were answered through the workshops. I commend the Alzheimer's Association for offering the public such a quality presentation.

Knowledge and truth are very important to me and, although knowing more about Alzheimer's was in one sense more alarming, I also found it consoling. Knowing what was happening to Mother's brain not only gave me understanding, but elicited a deeper compassion and a stronger desire to love her through it. It reminded me of John 8:32, *"and you will know the truth, and the truth will make you free."* There was a certain freedom that came from knowing what I was dealing with.

Subjects at the seminar covered an overview of dementia, management of Alzheimer's disease, research, and several workshops on specific difficulties pertaining to the disease. Most shocking and impressionable was a slide showing the brains of two different people. The brain on the left was normal. The one on the right displayed the atrophied brain of an Alzheimer's victim. The audience responded with an audible gasp, followed by quiet murmuring as we viewed the destruction of this disease on the brain and saw the devastation it left. The normal brain appeared full and firm, supple with slight creases; the diseased brain looked withered, shriveled up, and dried out like a prune with deep crevices across the surface. It reminded me of the results of a tornado sweeping through a town, leaving everything in its path in a state of ruin.

The presenters explained that Alzheimer's involves the neurological system, where brain cells become damaged, and as a result die. What this means is that the brain no longer communicates with itself. The nerve connections in the brain no longer function properly. First, memory is affected, then emotions, and finally, motor functions. I had trouble connecting that this was what my mother's brain looked like. No wonder she struggled so much with her thinking. Her brain had been severely compromised. It was a mass of tangles and disrupted signals.

Late in the day, as we awaited the next speaker, I turned in my chair to chat with the lady sitting behind me. She looked dismayed as she pondered all she had learned that day.

"It all seems so hopeless," she lamented. "There are no answers for this disease. I feel I have less hope now than when I came this morning." With those words expressed, our next speaker began, so I was compelled to turn my chair back to the front without an opportunity to respond to her disheartened outlook. Feeling the heaviness of her discouragement, her words weighed on my mind. With a silent prayer, I asked God how I could help her. He sent an immediate reply.

After the meeting, I turned to her again. "I've been thinking about what you said about feeling hopeless in your situation. May I share with you why I don't feel hopeless?"

"Yes, I'd like to hear," she said looking puzzled.

"You know, if all I had to base my hope on was the prognosis of Alzheimer's disease, I would feel distraught too. Doctors don't know what causes it and there is no cure. But my hope is not grounded in what happens with this disease. Rather, my hope is in the Lord, and I look to Him to strengthen me as I face this devastating illness in my mother.

Because of my faith in God and His promises, He has given me the assurance of knowing that when my mother leaves this world, she will be released from Alzheimer's disease. She will be whole and healthy, and her mind will function perfectly. My mother is also a woman of faith, so I'm certain she shares my confidence in God."

I went on to share some promises from the Bible which seemed to resonate with the lady's heart. "One of my favorites is from Revelation 21:4," I told her. *"And He will wipe away every tear from their eyes; and there will no longer be any death; there will no longer be any mourning, or crying, or pain; the first things have passed away."*

I reminded her that we can hold fast to the promises of Scripture. "They are there to give us a true hope, an expectation in the midst of life's pain and suffering. They are there to soothe the tender places in our hearts."

Encouraged by the warm look on her face, I continued talking to her about the Lord. I could tell she related to what I said. Our exchange lasted only a few minutes, but it was a special end to the day to have an opportunity to remind someone that we were not in this alone. God was there, and He cared. God could offer hope in the midst of an otherwise horrendous experience. As we left the auditorium, she thanked me for reminding her about the Lord and the power of prayer.

It had been a good day.

Hope

With this new era of life for my family, I hoped, even anticipated, that I would see God's hand in every aspect. Hope is an interesting word. In the original Hebrew language, it means "expectation" and "cord of attachment." God was our only hope as we faced the last days of Mother's time on earth. I wanted to stay closely attached to Him, expecting to see His hand in every situation that arose. As I adjusted to having my mother in Michigan, I learned to embrace new trials and look to God as the source of my only true hope.

Alzheimer's disease itself is hopeless from an earthly perspective. It cannot be reversed. Maybe someday that won't be so, but at that time, it was what it was. Today there are drugs which can help allay symptoms in the early stages, but there is still no cure. Yet, there was great hope in God's strength and grace as He unfolded His plan. Perhaps some diseases are left unresolved because that forces us to move out of the here and now and live on a different plane of trust in God. This life on earth is not all there is. God wants us to think eternally. The only sure hope we have is in God. All else can be shaken, but not the God who created us.

Do you know what Satan's #1 priority is? It is to destroy us, to separate us from our Creator. But how does He do it? Does he work on our faith? Joy? Peace? While he does to an extent, there is something more vulnerable that he goes after. The #1 priority of Satan is to destroy our hope because if he renders us hopeless, he automatically has our joy, our peace, and our faith. On the other hand, God has promised just the opposite. He has come to give us an abundant life (Jn. 10:10). In retrospect, I can say that the time I cared for my mother and watched after her needs turned out to be one of the richest experiences of my life. Why? Because I was aware that God was with me every step of the way.

Key Principle #24 - Look for hope and for opportunities to give others hope. During my mother's demise, it helped me to take my eyes off myself and focus on others and their problems. God frequently reminded me of who I am in Christ and how He is the answer to all life's crisis. It was good to have times of sharing hope with others.

I was reminded of II Corinthians 1:3-4 from the Living Bible. *"What a wonderful God we have - He is the Father of our Lord Jesus Christ, the source of every mercy, and the*

One who so wonderfully comforts and strengthens us in our hardships and trials. And why does He do this? So that when others are troubled, needing our sympathy and encouragement, we can pass on to them this same help and comfort God has given us." Powerful words! Words with purpose and meaning for all of life's difficulties.

48
Vain Imaginations and Anxiety

As Mother declined physically, we made many trips to the doctor's office. Since I had to make all of her medical decisions, I deliberated over each one, eager to make the correct choice. Doctors wanted to put her through many tests, and I carefully contemplated the necessity of each one. A specialist she visited ordered a test which I had personally undergone years before. Remembering my very painful experience caused me to agonize at the thought of allowing Mother to suffer the same procedure. I envisioned a troubling ordeal.

The thought of her being afflicted with such torturous pain led me to a number of stressful, sleepless nights. Prayer seemed empty and brought me no relief as my imagination went wild during the weeks prior to the test.

Finally the day came. As we sat in the doctor's office waiting for the culmination of this nightmare, I felt a measure of peace in the assurance that it would soon be over. Mother was oblivious as she happily paged through magazines in the waiting room. Soon she was escorted to the examining room. Being a private procedure, I remained in the waiting room trying not to focus on what she must be enduring, waiting for shrieks of pain.

All remained quiet.

Shortly Mother returned. Filled with tension I soberly asked her, "Well, how did it go, Mother?"

"Oh, it went fine," she replied with indifference.

"Was it terribly painful?" I squeamishly asked.

"No, not especially."

"It didn't hurt?" I asked in disbelief.

"No, I'm fine."

As I took in her unruffled response, I suddenly realized that I had agonized over something that never happened. I had lost sleep over a vain imagination. Refusing to trust God, He had allowed me to be consumed by my own fears. I had made the choice, and the only one who suffered that day was me.

Then the Lord brought to mind a verse that I later spent time contemplating. Isaiah 26:3, *"Thou wilt keep him in perfect peace whose mind is stayed on Thee because He trusteth in Thee."* (KJV) I looked up the word "mind" and in this context it means imagination, something framed that must be squeezed into a mold. As I considered these meanings, I began to see that it was not only my mind that needed to be stayed on or leaning into Christ but my imagination as well. Anxiety can trigger vain imaginations which in turn lead to fear. I needed to be sure the frame around my mind was Christ as the Holy Spirit renewed my mind day by day.

I heard a tape once on "True Imagination." It talked about imagination as a gift from God that must be corralled into conformity with Christ. Imagination is at its best when directed by the Holy Spirit. Anything other than that is a "vain" imagination and must be taken captive in obedience to Christ. We have multiple choices on a daily basis to either respond in the flesh or in the Spirit.

With that realization, I renewed my decision to choose to trust God with stressful areas in my life before they became obsessive. I found it was a process, one issue at a time. That night as I read the Bible, I felt Luke 21:34 was a word for me. *"Be careful, or your hearts will be weighed down with … the anxieties of life…."* (NIV)

I had been living with a heart that was overindulged or satiated with stress and anxiety. I found it interesting that anxiety was in the same sentence as drunkenness and dissipation, which is another word for indulgence. The cares and concerns of my life had weighed heavier than God ever intended. It was a word picture I could feel. Then Philippians 4:6 came to mind, reminding me to *"be anxious for nothing."*

I saw that I needed to be careful with issues of the heart, more aware of trusting the Lord in unknown situations. I saw the wasteful and destructive effect of vain imaginations and anxious thoughts. It didn't pay to keep my eye on the storm; peace came when I focused on the Lord.

Beth Moore, in her study of the book of James, asked her students to think of a problem situation they were presently dealing with. Then, she asked us to write down three ways to respond to the problem and how those reactions would affect the future.[7] My list of three responses to a problem were one, that I could complain and pout, making everyone around me miserable. Two, I could choose to be anxious and worried until my nerves were shot. Or three, I could choose the exhortation of James 1:2-3 and *"count it all joy,"* know- ing God would produce endurance in me. If I chose number three, the result would also include peace of mind, trust in God, and joy for others because joy is catching. It's really a choice and it's based on a core belief system. Again, I had some things to consider and an opportunity to allow God to produce some changes in my life.

49
Ups and Downs

S ince the test didn't bother Mother, she needed no time to recuperate. For that I was thankful. A beautiful day arrived and we took the opportunity to go on another walk. I loved taking her outside for some fresh air, but this time we walked only to the end of the street and back.

"I hear you have a blister, Mother. Where is it?"

"On my shoe," she answered.

"It's on your shoe?" I stifled a giggle. "Well, that's a funny place for a blister."

"Well yes, I guess it is," she agreed with a trace of amused interest.

I took her back to her house, both of us unaware that we had just taken our last walk together while she could actually walk. Within a few days she had a third TIA. Her head listed to the right; she became incoherent, babbled nonsense, looked weak, and had back pain. We decided to keep her at Fay's since the last two trips to the hospital had resulted in merely waiting out the attack anyway.

In the midst of her discomfort, we had a sweet visit. "What shall we read from the Bible, Mother? How about we read the part where Jesus comes back?" Turning to I Thessalonians 4, I read to her about the rapture and how we will one day be caught up together in the clouds with Jesus, to always be with the Lord. Verse 18 says, *"Therefore comfort one another with these words."*

"Mother, are you comforted by these words?" She nodded that she was. We read I Corinthians 15 and I told her about the new body she would have when she went to be with Jesus, a perfect body with no more pain and a perfect mind. We talked about the hope we have in the Lord and the mansion He had prepared for her (Jn.14:1-3). When I got to John 14:6, I was encouraged as she recited after me each section of that verse, even though a thin whisper. *"Jesus said to him, 'I am the way, and the truth, and the life; no one comes to the Father, but through Me.'"*

"Mother, one day you will go to live with Jesus. There will be no more pain and no more tears. Isn't that wonderful?" She nodded yes. I sang "What a Friend We Have in Jesus," then followed with some Christmas carols which seemed appropriate even though the month was April. While I sang "O Come All Ye Faithful" and "Joy to the World," Mother mouthed the words, her voice growing fainter. We rejoiced in the Lord and prayed together. It was a treasured moment I will cherish forever.

I stopped in to see Mother again that week and stayed to give Fay a break by feeding her dinner. She was too weak to feed herself. She ate well as usual, but continued to lose weight. One of the odd symptoms of Alzheimer's in the later stages is that the patient loses weight regardless of how much food they consume.

The next day Mother rallied and sat in her chair. Fay optimistically announced that Mother was gaining strength. I continued to be so thankful for Fay and all that she did for Mother. She truly went the extra mile. Some weeks before, Fay and I had a talk about whether Fay felt she could keep Mother till the end. In the event that she chose not to, I had looked at a nursing home alternative, although I still wasn't ready to go that route. Mother had moved so many times already, but I knew the day might come when Fay would consider it too much to continue caring for her.

As I approached the subject, I didn't know what to expect. Fay, however, had already considered it and her reply was, "Of course I'll keep your mother to the end."

It turns out she had a sister who had endured early onset Alzheimer's and had consequently died sooner than normal. Fay knew what to expect. "I am committed to your mother's care,

Betsy, and want her to stay with me even as she deteriorates physi-cally." I left revived by the good news that Mother was welcome to stay. It was a tremendous relief and an answer to prayer.

Although Mother had rallied the day before, things often change quickly with the feeble. While grocery shopping, I ran into Stacy, Fay's assistant. She gave me a bad report. "Your mother is weakening again, Betsy. It takes three of us to get her around. She's really too frail to get out of bed. She has a temperature, a backache, and her head is off to the right again." I was touched when she added that she and her children prayed for Mother every day.

As she continued naming things wrong with Mother, I had a sense that this time Mother was truly slipping toward her eternal destination. She was dying. It scared me to say it. I'd never watched anyone die. My father had passed away seventeen years before, but I had lived so far away that I only saw him twice before he passed, and I wasn't present on the day he died. I hadn't gone through the process with him.

I wanted Mother out of her pain and misery, but we had bonded again over the past year and a half. It amazed me that I could feel so close to a person who could no longer communicate, who had, in essence, lost her personality. Yet she remained so sweet and non-complaining, endearing her caretakers, including me. As I left her room after a visit that evening, I paused to look back and whispered to myself, "Good night, Mother. I wonder if you'll be there tomorrow."

Reminiscing

Mother lay peacefully in her bed as I left, oblivious to her surroundings, quiet in her spirit. I mourned for my mother that night and began to reminisce back to the earlier stages of Alzheimer's when she had been into everything. Drawers a chaotic mess, cassette tapes with the tape pulled out in a pile, playing cards tucked into magazines and greeting cards, bits of paper stacked here and there. Fay had said then, that Mother was the hardest person she had ever cared for. Her agitation had been like hurricane force winds with violent flashes of lightening and roaring thunder. So severe had it been that, out of pity, we had slightly medicated her to give her soul a rest. Now, all was quiet, the storm had passed, and calmness enveloped her soul.

Over the years, I've missed the blessing of elderly people in my life. I never knew any of my grandparents. Miles separated us as well as their apparent lack of interest in relationship. In my younger years, I had a grandmotherly babysitter, Grandma Bracken. We had a warm relationship.

I remember another older lady, Mary, who attended one of my Bible studies years ago. She walked with a cane and always carried a glass of water with a straw. She had a dry mouth and sipped water all day long. Mary told stories that impacted my life. Several years later, I visited her in a nursing home. Expecting the same bright person, it surprised me to see her old and dying. "Mary, remember Jesus. He loves you," I encouraged. She nodded her affirmation.

Thinking of my mother's pending death reminded me of my own mortality too. Why do we Americans consider death an almost unapproachable subject? Why do we find it so offensive? Other cultures aren't so closed to this idea. Perhaps it's the painful thought of losing someone we love. Perhaps it's the invincible feeling we Americans have. We're like John Wayne, indestructible. Or perhaps it's because our culture has fallen away from God and many feel this life is all there is, so it must be gripped with a tight hold. How sad to miss the hope of Jesus and the promise of a better world to come. This life is not all there is. We were created with a God given drive to live, not to die. It's sin that brings death to mankind. We're hard wired to seek life, and God's desire is that we do live forever with Him.

50
Back to the Hospital

Within days, once again an ambulance had to be called to take Mother to the hospital. We couldn't get her out of bed. Complications on several levels had taken a toll on her body. Alzheimer's had destroyed her brain and, in the process, communication from the brain to body parts became jumbled. As a result, some of her bodily functions diminished further. Some organs had ceased to know how to operate at all. Mother's bowels completely forgot how to work, so impaction followed.

None of the things she was hospitalized for was life threatening, but my emotions still fluttered with each episode. I asked the doctor what his prognosis was. He answered that it was possible she could live for years in this condition. I made the decision to begin assuming that Mother might live a long time and that she might frequently be in and out of the hospital.

Her roommate this time had undergone an operation. I noticed she had a rosary in her hand, so I started a conversation with her. God gave me an opportunity to pray for her and encourage her in her recuperation. Again, I was thankful for the chance to reach out to another suffering soul.

Mother was in the hospital for about a week this time. When she returned to Fay's, it shocked me to find a large black sore on her heel. My first thought was that she had gangrene. Frantic, I ran to get Fay. She was out, but her husband explained that Mother had come home from the hospital with a bedsore. I had never seen one before and found the sight appalling and painful to look at.

I later read that bedsores are not just a blister or abrasion. They are rotting of the flesh so that it turns black. They can occur when a patient is not properly turned to different positions while lying in bed for extended periods of time. The pressure on one part of the body will eventually cause the skin to break down and form a bedsore. I wondered if Mother's sore could have been avoided if she had been adjusted in her bed periodically. But then again, her skin was so frail, almost translucent, and may have succumbed anyway. At any rate, we took her to the doctor the next day for treatment, and he began the process of debriding, (pronounced debreeding). This involved the removal of dead or damaged tissue and cleansing of the wound. Too weak to walk, we carried Mother to and from the car for each appointment. My poor frail mother was enduring yet another trial.

Worship in the Midst of Trial

This episode marked one of my lower points. The process of dying had become a cruel taskmaster. It was relentless in its ways. I felt like I was running a race and losing. Each time I caught up, a new ailment appeared. We ran with it, got it under control, only to find something else was wrong.

Death is a destroyer, and I was watching Mother's physical body being destroyed bit by bit. Her mind was almost completely gone and her body was deteriorating rapidly. We plugged one hole and another sprang open. We did the best we could but it wasn't good enough. The process was harsh and relentless, raw and cruel. At times, only the tiny light of Jesus at the end of the tunnel made it bearable.

Though her mental and physical body ceased to function properly, though medications rarely worked, though edema had swollen her feet and an ugly bedsore persisted, though she needed a wheelchair and had forgotten how to walk, though she couldn't communicate and her mind was gone, I chose to declare the words of a heartfelt hymn written by Horatio Spafford, "It is well, it is well with my soul." Yes, that day I made a volitional choice to bless the name of the Lord. David, in the book of Psalms often spoke to his soul, telling it how to respond, that it should bless the Lord. I would do the same.

For some reason one of my favorite Scriptures is Habakkuk 3:17-19. *"Though the fig tree should not blossom, and there be no fruit on the vines, though the yield of the olive should fail, and the fields produce no food, though the flock should be cut off from the fold, and there be no cattle in the stalls, yet I will exult in the Lord. I will rejoice in the God of my salvation. The Lord God is my strength, and He has made my feet like hinds' feet, and makes me walk on my high places."*

I looked up the meaning of high places in one of my study books. It means a place of worship, an altar to the Lord. As I thought about this, I realized, that as circumstances grew more difficult, God wanted me to offer Him thanks, rejoicing, praise, and worship. As I did this, a spiritual altar was built to His name. With my offering, God strengthened me that I might endure and go on. I believe that God inhabits the praises of His people. Surely, the Presence of the Lord was with me as I worshipped Him in the midst of each new trial. Times of worship became times of refreshing, times to refocus.

Fresh Air

To my amazement, Mother rallied again and now spent time sitting in her chair. As she could no longer walk on her own, I rented a wheelchair from the hospital. That made it possible to take her out for fresh air. Our first outing lasted half an hour. She smiled in anticipation of being outdoors again. It was spring, a beautiful time in Michigan. Magnolia trees bloomed with their soft pink flowers; tulips and daffodils made their bright red and yellow appearance; the smell of freshly mowed grass permeated the air. The rigors of winter's harsh weather were past, replaced with warm, gentle breezes, and days that were inviting.

"Take deep breaths, Mother, and enjoy the sweet smells of spring," I prompted. I pointed out various flowering trees and bushes and encouraged her to savor the beauty of God's creation. I walked slowly, pushing her in a wheelchair as we both drank in the warmth and sunshine.

Later, as we returned to the house, Mother looked up at me with soft eyes and whispered, "I love you, Betsy. You're so important to me." She fought back tears. I think we both did. This was the first display of emotion I had seen in months. A window of clarity, a shaft of light had beckoned those thoughts to pass from her lips. I was awed that she spoke in clear sentences. This would be remembered as a precious moment of lucidity from the mother I had loved for so many years. Some part of my real mother was still alive.

Several days later, she displayed emotion again. Disturbed this time, I detected fear. By playing twenty questions, even though she could not verbalize her concerns, I determined that she again needed reassurance about her memory loss, difficulty understanding, and general thinking glitches. Although she couldn't really express these things, I went on instinct that this was the cause of her distress. Speaking to her quietly soothed her, and as we prayed together her soul settled a bit. It was like comforting a child. Words have such power to pacify or alarm. Proverbs 18:21 offers this thought. *"Death and life are in the power of the tongue...."* (KJV) My prayer was that my words would be life to Mother.

These two displays of emotion revealed to me that, though her mind failed to function properly, she still felt at least fleeting emotion. By now, I was thankful for any evidence of my mother's essence.

51
Difficult Decisions

The early summer months passed with minor ups and downs, and then August arrived. Mother's strength diminished greatly and she ate less and less. Her diet dwindled to liquids, but soon she forgot how to suck from a straw. With a cup and straw no longer options, Bill suggested Fay give her water with a turkey baster. This idea met with some success. At least it kept her mouth moist, and she was more comfortable.

A difficult decision was on the horizon. Mother was clearly dying. Whereas I had anticipated that she would eventually die of a heart attack or a stroke, we now faced an unexpected foe. Mother was dying from a bedsore! With her immune system waning (also connected with Alzheimer's), one of her bedsores had become infected and wasn't responding to a strong antibiotic.

We had three possible choices. One would be plastic surgery with skin grafts which would involve three weeks in the hospital. Since her bedsore was the result of a hospital stay, we assumed she would probably develop more with that option. Considering the weakened state of her skin, we thought she would likely come home in worse shape than when she entered the hospital. The second alternative would be a hospital stay with antibiotics given through an I.V. along with intubations for nutrition. This would have bought time for her, but for what reason? Why put her through all that? The third alternative would be to keep her comfortable at Fay's and try another round of oral antibiotics. We chose option three.

Amazingly, her body responded to the medication this time and the infection cleared up. However, even with a high protein drink and as much liquid as she would receive, Mother remained malnourished and emaciated. Soon it became necessary to engage the services of a visiting nurse who came two to four times a week to tend to the more difficult physical issues. Fay was thankful for the extra help.

To add to the complications, Mother's only communication consisted of a raspy, whispered yes or no. She was clearly in further decline.

An ardent opponent of euthanasia, I wrestled with an aspect of this topic for many weeks, though not with the idea of taking proactive steps to end her life. That never crossed my mind and would have been against my belief system. My concern was more in the area of how much do you do for a dying person? What constitutes enough? When is it euthanasia, and when is it just time to let go? What would God want me to do to help her? What would I want done for myself in the same situation?

After much prayer, I did what I would want someone to do for me. I, personally, would not want to be kept alive with tubes if I were elderly and clearly near death. To my knowledge, Mother did not have a DNR (Do Not Resuscitate) order to fall back on, so this decision lay on my shoulders. My question was this: Why buy her body earthly time when meeting the Lord would end all the pain and discomfort and be a better place for her? There is a time to live and a time to die. We never withheld food or drink. Mother's body just became incapable of responding.

God comforted me with a verse from the Psalms. *"Precious in the sight of the Lord is the death of His godly ones"* (Ps. 116:15). I knew He was waiting to receive my mother into His loving arms, and I believed she was ready to meet Him face to face.

Life Goes On

About this time, Cynthia had planned to leave for a five week opera tour in Southeast Asia. Before going, she came for one last visit with Mother. We both suspected Mother would die while she was away. She brought a tape for Mother which she had made of hymns and Christmas songs. It was beautifully done and surely comforted my soul. Mother listened, we think, but showed no response.

Shortly after Cynthia's visit, our family left for a week-long trip to a cabin on a lake in northern Michigan. We left a phone number with Fay but were thankful no call came. It was a much needed week of family relaxation and fun. We spent time canoeing, reading, climbing dunes, and hiking. After this welcome vacation, we returned home refreshed.

I visited Mother as soon as we arrived home and found her hanging onto life by a thread. As I had on other occasions, I read her the first verses of II Corinthians 5. *"For we know that if the earthly tent which is our house is torn down, we have a building from God, a house not made with hands, eternal in the heavens. For indeed in this house we groan, longing to be clothed with our dwelling from heaven."* With those words, Mother gave a groan. I didn't think much of it until I went on reading.

"For indeed while we are in this tent, we groan, being burdened. . . ." As she again groaned, I felt this was her spirit responding to the very thing I was reading. Mother had dwindled to the point where her ability to converse was almost gone. With only rare responses now, she was in and out of consciousness most of the time. I still chose to speak to her spirit by reading Scripture to her. To me her groans were an indication that though we could no longer communicate person to person,

because of Jesus, we could communicate spirit to spirit. So I spoke to her spirit.

"For we walk by faith, not by sight - we are of good courage, I say, and prefer rather to be absent from the body and to be at home with the Lord" (II Cor. 5:7-8).

"Mother, you'll be with Jesus soon and the groaning will be over."

Key Principle #25 - Read Scripture even if there is no response. It's good and profitable to communicate to a dying person's spirit. I found the best and most fulfilling way to communicate with Mother at this time was by speaking directly to her spirit. As Christians we are spiritual beings with the Holy Spirit indwelling us. Though she no longer had the capacity to respond verbally, I felt an assurance in my heart that her soul and spirit would respond to the Word of God. So I fed her spirit with Scripture.

I pondered how important honest responses are to us as human beings. At times, any response from another human being is better than no response. We are social beings and we need each other. I felt some strange emotions when Mother didn't respond to me anymore. I began to think about the pain, rejection, and suffering many children and spouses encounter when family neglects to reply. Some even confuse family members with passive aggressive responses. Emotion gets stuffed down when there is no reply, no affirmation, and no approval in a relationship.

Bill spoke with a friend who lived a great distance from her mother who had Alzheimer's. Her mother was in the last stages of the disease and could no longer communicate. Although there were many family members living nearby, they had all chosen not to visit her anymore because she rarely recognized them and couldn't carry on a conversation. They felt awkward around her, not knowing what to say. The ensuing silence was uncomfortable. Bill told her to encourage them to speak to her spirit, to read Scripture, sing hymns, and pray during their time together. He shared how that would minister to her soul.

Most family members want to do something but may feel their best efforts are useless in the end stage of Alzheimer's disease. Guilt and frustration mingle because they want to be helpful but don't know what to do. Speaking to Mother's spirit became a natural and comfortable thing for me. I think it ministered to both of us and gave us a special bond.

During those final months, watching the agony Mother endured, I caught myself wishing she would soon pass out of this life and into eternity. Her life had become so burdensome to her. I often prayed that God would be merciful and take her home to be with Him, that her suffering and mine would end. Sometimes I felt like a monster for thinking such a thing. Yet, I dreamed about the emotional relief that would come in our lives when this was all over. Only someone emotionally involved with a victim of a harsh disease will understand the feelings I had. I loved my mother and wanted the best for her, but at the same time, I longed to live without the constant weight of concern that is ever present when someone you love is suffering.

Her life had become one of misery, always laying there, empty eyes, bed sores, infections, body functions ceasing one by one. The experts say Alzheimer's victims usually die from pneumonia or some other infection. I wondered what would finally take Mother.

When I had these thoughts, I also knew that the days Mother spent on this earth were ordained by God. "*. . . And in Thy book they were all written, the days that were ordained for me, when as yet there was not one of them*" (Ps. 139:16). God had a perfect plan and Mother would survive until God called her home. I tried to rest in that thought.

Near the end, one day I found Mother in a state of agitation, not exactly thrashing on the bed but clearly uncomfortable. I tried to engage her in some question and answer time to see if I could discern what was wrong. Semi-conscious, she was only able to whimper a muffled yes or no on this occasion.

"Are you feeling okay today, Mother?" (Indistinguishable mumble)

"Do you hurt anywhere?" No answer.

"Where does it hurt?" Still no response, just restless movement. It used to be I could ask her to point to the body part that bothered her, and she would comply with some sort of indication. She could no longer do that.

So I pointed to various body parts and asked, "Is it your stomach?"

"No," she groaned.

"Is it your back?"

I heard a faint, "No."

"A headache?"

Again after a pause, a muted, "No," was voiced.

I continued to inquire, "Your neck?"

"Yes," she weakly sighed. It had been an ordeal to figure out what was wrong, and she was clearly exhausted from the process. Her arthritic neck bothered her. She'd already taken her pain medication. So, we waited. I couldn't do anything for her.

Then, even that occasional, meager communication waned. She slept a lot, and days went by when she rarely woke up. She lay in bed all the time now, occasionally awakening, with glazed eyes and no acknowledgement of me or the world around her.

Eventually, the day came when she forgot how to swallow. Research I had done explained that this was one of the final symptoms of Alzheimer's. Mother continued to be a "classic textbook case," right to the end.

Semi-conscious most of the time, she developed deep lung congestion; yet even with no response, we continued to have some sweet times. By faith, I believed that I could still speak Scripture, and that it would minister to her. God's Word does not return empty or void. It's rich and full, and accomplishes the purposes for which God sends it. So, I continued to feed her spirit, even in view of her severe state of health.

I read Psalm 23, prayed with her, and sang some Psalms, hymns, and spiritual songs. As I sang "I Will Celebrate," I recalled that, months earlier, we had talked about what she would like to do for her birthday. Mother loved to dance and she said she wanted a party. Now I told her she would soon be dancing before the Lord. That party she had wanted for her birthday was about to happen. No more tears or suffering, her mind restored, her body whole again, and a happy smile awaited her. And, perhaps, a special dance awaited her with a very unique and extraordinary "Someone."

The next morning, August 20, 1991, a warm Michigan summer day, our son, Mike, and I took a long bike ride and had lunch at a restaurant in a nearby town. Arriving home mid afternoon, Bill met us with the news that Mother had died at 12:15 P.M. While the visiting nurse had done her procedures, Mother just fell asleep.

It was over.

Months and years of anguish and trial had met their end. "Thank you, Lord."

I cried, releasing all the pain and emotion we both had endured through the ravages of this disease in every stage. Blessed be the name of the Lord who poured out His mercy on my mother.

"For the Lord Himself will descend from heaven with a shout, with the voice of the archangel and with the trumpet of God, and the dead in Christ will rise first. Then we who are alive and remain will be caught up together with them in the clouds to meet the Lord in the air, and so we shall always be with the Lord," (I Thess. 4:16-17).

"Well Mother, I'll meet you in the air. Our hope is in the Lord."

52
A Difficult Question

Along the path of ministering to a person with a fatal ailment, whether Alzheimer's or some other disease that has no cure, it may seem normal to ask, "Why?" Why does my loved one have Alzheimer's? Why is there no cure? Why do victims act the way they do? Why isn't there a drug to control this ailment? I've read articles over the years that have blamed the cause of Alzheimer's on everything from aluminum exposure to lack of mental stimulation, from chemicals in the environment to our compromised, processed food supply. You may have asked some "why" questions yourself and felt confused, overwhelmed or helpless at the lack of answers.

With my mother, I could have allowed that question to eat at me until it chewed me up and ate me alive, metaphorically speaking, of course. To answer the question as to why Mother had Alzheimer's, I can only say this: I don't know. Nobody really knows. There comes a point with some questions in life where we hit a wall. There is no imminent answer.

I recently watched a TV show called, "Who Do You Think You Are?" It's a show put on by Ancestry.com where the genealogies of celebrities are traced back several generations. As a black celebrity investigated his ancestry, it was revealed that there were slaves in his lineage. When he discovered that the Census in those days did not include the names of slaves, he hit a wall in his research. There would be no way to continue tracing his family of origin.

In thinking about Alzheimer's, I had to remember that God always knows the answer to every question. The day may come when He reveals to scientists exactly what causes Alzheimer's and how to cure it, but for now, we've hit a wall.

In the TV show, they did a DNA test on the black man, and interestingly, they found a match for a cousin in Africa. It was one more step for him as the threads of his past were unraveled. In the same way, God through science may someday reveal more about Alzheimer's. But it hasn't happened yet.

Meanwhile, the key to peace of mind when addressing the issue of Alzheimer's is to remind ourselves that God is Sovereign. He knows the beginning from the end. We are always on His mind and in His heart. As we seek Him, we can know his unconditional love now and for all eternity.

If God would ask us a question, I think it might be this. "Will you trust me in the darkest hour when no answers are apparent, when things seem hidden, dark or shadowed, when nothing makes sense, or will you only trust Me when you can see things clearly?" It's an imposing question I had to ask myself. A question requiring reliance on God while abiding in the unknown. In the end, isn't that what God wants from us? Simple faith, belief that He can be trusted even when things don't seem logical, even when no answer is on the horizon. Proverbs 3:5-6 has this encouragement. *"Trust in the LORD with all your heart, and do not lean on your own understanding. In all your ways acknowledge Him, and He will make your paths straight."*

Something to Ponder

We have all seen beautiful tapestries that hang in museums or homes. Have you ever had occasion to look at the back side of one? I used to do needlepoint which on a much smaller scale will illustrate the same idea. As I wove various colors into the design I was creating, had I just focused on the back side of the craft, I would have been too discouraged to continue sewing. One color crossed another with no symmetrical explanation. Black strands were layered and interwoven with red, yellow or green. Knots appeared everywhere a thread had been tied off. Nothing made sense on the back side. It was a menagerie of sewing insanity. No picture emerged, just a cacophony of colors and hanging threads.

But on the front side, a pleasant and enjoyable picture began to materialize. Colors blended in a way where black yarns highlighted the brighter colors, making them even more striking in appearance. No knots appeared on the front side. Each strand settled as a needed part of the whole. It made sense. It offered a satisfying, if not pleasing, image.

I liken this to the time I spent looking after my mother. If I had looked separately at all the events that made up the back side of the tapestry of Mother's final days, it would have made no sense. Many colors were interwoven in Mother's life. She had many brightly colored days, but as her life waxed dim, gray, brown, and black colors were added. Perhaps those darker colors, in the end, were used as part of a greater plan to highlight the glory of God, His Majesty and the wonder of who He is. When seen on the other side of eternity, God will surely be glorified because He will have taken the ravages of Mother's final days and used them to underscore the amazing transformation that is now hers to behold. He has transferred her out of this temporary state of mental and physical devastation, out of the darkness that surrounded her final days. He has replaced it with a perfect, new body, and a whole, sound mind which she will have for all eternity. This life is but a passing moment. Paul says it well in Romans 8:18, *"For I consider that the sufferings of this present time are not worthy to be compared with the glory that is to be revealed to us."*

What awesome glory is His for displaying this transforming power! The grandeur and brilliance of His final work in Mother's life, His redemptive work, outshines anything that could have been her lot here on earth. True, we did not see all this while she was on this side with us. But by faith, we know we will one day see Mother as the woman God created her to be. What, on this earth, looked like a dismal end was really just the beginning. I can almost hear the majestic crescendo of heavenly chords as Mother took her place amidst the splendor of the living God, all the threads in perfect harmony, united and overlaid with the brilliance of God's amazing love. This is my sure hope, my unshakeable anchor. *"Now faith is the assurance of things hoped for, the conviction of things not seen."* (Heb. 11:1)

Writing

Although the year and a half that Mother lived in Michigan was one of the hardest times of my life, it was also one of the most rewarding. It turned out to be the adventure in God that I had prayed it would be. God met me at every turn. He answered prayers, gave me direction, encouraged, and comforted me in specific ways throughout Mother's illness. As I drew close to Him, He drew close to me, just as He promised.

Writing details of Mother's journey through Alzheimer's, and recording my feelings and experiences, offered me a creative and healing outlet. It became the bedrock material for this book. I did a lot of writing on other subjects during that time as well and an in-depth study of end time theology. For months, I read numbers of books and articles and listened to tapes and speakers on prophesy. Studying future things during Mother's illness was no mistake. As I focused on this subject, God used it to give me perspective. Life here on earth is not all that God offers.

As I read about the dead in Christ rising first and we who remain joining Him in the air, I recognized that the downhill struggle Mother and I experienced was not the end of the story. Death has no victory for the believer. I was able to let her go, knowing we will one day be raised to be with the Lord and each other, forever. There is great hope in that knowledge. Mother has already gone from life, through death, to life. One day I will join her.

God used the creative activity of writing as spiritual therapy during an otherwise strenuous season of life. He loves balance. While Mother went downhill, God brought new life, energy, and inspiration to me through writing and research.

Alzheimer's seemed to win, but the Lord is the final authority over all disease and He says it has been conquered and will one day bow to Him. We are victors and conquerors over death and illness through the blood of Jesus Christ (I Cor.15:54-57).

God chose not to heal Mother on this side, but her healing became reality the moment she left this earth and stepped into the glory of eternity. Hallelujah!

53
Twenty-five Key Principles

Throughout this book, I have listed twenty-five "Key Principles" which I found helpful for walking in triumph in the midst of a trial. God has always meant for us to be triumphant as we walk through the trials of life. He didn't select some circumstances and say there's no possibility of being victorious in this situation. No, He has provided all that we need to be more than conquerors in every test in life. However, in many situations, we have to take the opportunities He gives us. This is where we become not only hearers but doers of the Word (James 1:22).

I heard a story about a girl who had taken a Bible class in an effort to break free from bondages in her life. Afterward, she lamented that she was still held captive to the oppressive issues that bound her. The teacher wisely asked her if she had done the things she had learned in the study, or had she just read and studied them. With that, the girl realized that while she had enjoyed the class and written out all the homework assignments, she had never put any of it into practice.

James 1:22 articulates that if we only hear and don't follow up with doing, we are deluding or deceiving ourselves. We can't expect change to happen without some doing and that takes the power of the Holy Spirit.

Through walking with my mother in her Alzheimer's tragedy, I realized anew that grace is offered beyond our salvation experience. Christianity involves the ability and the power to live life at a higher level through the Holy Spirit. Ephesians 3:16-19 says, *"that He would grant you, according to the riches of His glory, to be strengthened with power through His Spirit in the inner man...."*

For me, the twenty-five principles were walked out through the power and anointing of the Holy Spirit, along with God's abiding grace. The principles are geared toward the dignity of the Alzheimer's victim, our responses, and realizing who we are in Christ. Following is a recap of the principles and how they helped me live as more than a survivor of a sad circumstance. Through God's personal involvement each day, I found He could be depended on to keep me in perspective, and even prosper me, in spite of what went on around me. As I walked in the adventure and holy calling that God had ordained for me, I learned to focus on Jesus and call on Him to lead me into victory. He can be trusted to do the same for you.

Key Principles

1. Preserve dignity and integrity at any cost. (Page 34) I tried to include Mother in as much of the decision making as her capabilities would allow.

2. Be sure to initiate affection. (Page 34) I was liberal with hugging her, holding her hand, rubbing her back, and telling her I loved her.

3. Let love be your guide to maintaining peace and unity. (Page 34) I made a commitment not to argue and to choose wholesome attitudes. I was reminded of the Scripture that says, *"...Do your work heartily as unto the Lord...* (Col. 3:23). I decided to try to treat Mother as I would treat the Lord.

4. Remember Alzheimer's victims are not hard of hearing. (Page 35) I was careful with what I said in her presence. In her paranoid state, Mother often thought people were talking about her.

5. Offer prayer and read with her. (Page 35) Spiritual nourishment was an important ingredient. Praying and reading the Bible together helped unify all the other principles and brought God's perspective into our relationship.

6. Spot check your mindset. (Page 49) By frequently examining my thoughts and attitudes, I was able to make adjustments in my choice of responses.

7. Realize God is in control and can be trusted even in the unknown. (Page 69) When things seemed out of control by sight, I reminded myself that God was still on the throne and that He still had a perfect plan which He was unfolding for us.

8. Accept odd behavior and humor her. (Page 84) Fighting unusual behavior would have caused frustration for both of us. Changing my expectations was a key to accepting her behavior.

9. Pray diligently for every need. (Page 116) Leaning on God through prayer for every decision was a key to walking in victory. Through prayer, I had the privilege of seeing God move in many ways on Mother's behalf.

10. Be aware of character qualities God is developing in you, especially attitudes and choices. (Page 151) God used the circumstances of my life to build His character into me. Being aware of this process, I could make attitude choices to cooperate with what He was building.

11. Accept suffering as a part of life, and choose a heart of service. (Page 163) If one thing is promised in Scripture, it is suffering. In the midst of suffering there were opportunities to serve.

12. Cooperate with God, and consider seeing the situation as an "Adventure in God." (Page 166) Whatever this situation brought, I decided I would consider it an occasion to walk by faith, trusting that God had a plan and purpose. I knew God's ultimate purpose was for our good.

13. Lean on Jesus and His Word, and allow the Holy Spirit to lead. (Page 171) Time in the Bible profited me on a daily basis. I found strength and peace through God's Word. It became especially important when I felt overwhelmed by the endless responsibilities.

14. Give time for adjustment. (Page 174) Sometimes, things changed in Mother's life at a fast pace. I needed to be understanding of her emotions during these difficult times. Her mind had trouble assimilating even the simplest changes. It helped her when I took time to explain.

15. Change the subject when needed. (Page 182) Some subjects were quite disturbing for Mother. I had to become aware of which ones caused turmoil. When these subjects came up, I tried to change the course of the conversation to something more neutral.

16. Savor sweet moments. (Page 183) I wanted some good memories of Mother's last years, not just memories of drudgery and fighting a disease. Sweet moments became a valuable well spring of peace and contentment for both of us in the midst of her struggles.

17. Listening is important. (Page 186) I learned from Dr. Brothers that listening affirmed Mother's dignity. He made no verbal judgments which would have exasperated her. Rather, he listened intently with consideration of her feelings.

18. Alleviate guilt by setting realistic priorities and choosing to live by them. (Page 193) Guilt comes when we think we're not doing enough. Once I determined realistic parameters of "enough," and received Bill's support, guilt was alleviated.

19. Give yourself permission to laugh. (Page 197) Seeing humor in situations kept me in balance and provided much needed release. I tried to keep visits with Mother light hearted and fun, and we often joked with each other. Thankfully, until close to the end, she was still adept at thinking of witty things to say.

20. Take time to be thankful. (Page 210) I found that in the midst of troubling situations, no matter how bleak they appeared, there was always something for which to be thankful.

21. Allow time to grieve. (Page 225) Grieving is a natural God given release for the pain and the sense of loss we feel. I had not realized that a person could grieve while someone was still alive. I grieved in increments as Mother slowly lost her mind to Alzheimer's.

22. Consider caretaking a holy calling from God. (Page 243) I believe God ordained my caretaking responsibilities toward my mother, and I regarded them as a holy calling. This thought gave me perspective. God had made me a steward of my mother's life.

23. Find a support group. (Page 245) A support group provided a place where I could share with people who could empathize because they were in a similar situation. They understood. Many of the members offered suggestions for handling issues that had worked for them.

24. Look for hope and opportunities to give others hope. (Page 287) During my mother's demise, it helped me to take my eyes off myself and focus on giving others hope in God. God frequently reminded me of who I am in Christ and how He is the answer to all life's crisis.

25. Read Scripture even if there is no response. (Page 309) Though Mother no longer had the capacity to respond verbally, I felt an assurance in my heart that her soul and spirit would respond to the Word of God. So, I fed her spirit with Scripture.

Appendix 1
Helpful Suggestions

During my mother's illness, we had to make many decisions. We learned some things that I would like to pass on, answers that would have helped if we had known about them beforehand. Most of it I had to flesh out as we traveled our journey with my mother and Bill's parents. We will use this list to help our children know our wishes when we become elderly and possibly incapacitated. The following inventory includes legal issues as well as practical suggestions that might be helpful for your consideration. I make no claim to being a legal advisor, so whatever suggestions I give that helped us should be critiqued and confirmed by your own attorney.

1. Durable Power of Attorney for Medical and Financial Affairs

One of the toughest issues in the final years was in regard to authority to handle both medical and financial matters for Mother. To facilitate this, I needed Durable Power of Attorney in those two areas. That would allow me jurisdiction over her financial and medical affairs. These two separate documents are designed to help with the legal issues of an incapacitated person.

At first, we obtained a simple Power of Attorney which Mother signed. At the time, I didn't know that document wouldn't be enough, and that it would end when Mother became incapacitated. When we later realized that Mother was incapable of taking care of herself, she and I visited a lawyer again to get Durable Power of Attorney.

If possible, Durable Power of Attorney should be obtained while the person is still lucid, yet it need not be exercised until the need arises. By the time we obtained these for Mother, she could only sign an X for her name. Out of respect for her, it would have been better to do this when she was still able to be part of the decision, but we did find that the X was accepted in Michigan. Each state may be different, so it's best to contact a local attorney regarding this issue.

Handling financial matters such as signing checks, depositing or withdrawing funds, investment decisions, insurance issues, property concerns, annuities, debt, and things of this nature were easily accomplished once we obtained a Financial Durable Power of Attorney. Likewise, having a Medical Durable Power of Attorney allowed me to make medical decisions when Mother was no longer able to take care of her own health matters.

It's also important to know that Durable Power of Attorney is rendered invalid at the time of death. This makes things like cashing checks with their name difficult without having a valid, in state Will or Trust and an executor of the estate specified.

2. Have a Will Drawn Up

If the person doesn't have a Will, be sure to have one drawn up while they can still make choices. Much grief and many financial complications can result from not having a Will. Laws differ according to each state, so again, talking to a local attorney can alleviate this from being a difficulty later on.

3. Living Trust

Ask an attorney about the advisability of putting invest-ments into a Living Trust and appointing an executor to the Trust. We did this, and it saved most of Mother's investments from going through probate. Probate can be very expensive and time consuming. A Living Trust can be drawn up early in life and is a wonderful protection for family members. Laws change regarding trusts, so it's good to check with an attor-ney. It is also critical that all deeds, accounts, stocks, titles, and beneficiaries listed are current and correct. If there is a trust, all assets need to be titled to the trust.

4. Bank Account

Open a joint bank account for ease in handling financial matters, and have the statements sent to your address. You can then pay bills, receive checks, and manage that account.

5. Social Security Payments

Make arrangements for Social Security payments to be paid directly into the joint bank account. Durable Financial Power of Attorney will allow you to do that. At the end, be certain that a Death Certificate is sent to Social Security so that payments will stop.

6. Bill Payments

When you begin taking over all the bills, have them transferred to your address. Alzheimer's victims may lose or hide mail. It is prudent to have all their mail delivered to your home, so you can deliver personal letters and assist with opening and reading them.

7. Investments

Obtain a list of all income and assets. For convenience, consider transferring investments to an investment broker in your town. This can be done through your Durable Financial Power of Attorney. Again, make sure these are all titled correctly.

8. Housing Needs

Find out their desire for living arrangements. Earlier in her life, Mother had expressed that she hoped I would never have to put her in a nursing home. Knowing this, I asked the Lord to provide an alternative solution. He provided the adult foster care home. There are several alternatives to choose from today. Nursing homes, adult foster care homes, in home help, or living with a relative are some of the viable options.

If you choose the latter, you can also take advantage of visiting nurses (covered by Medicare), hospice care, senior day care centers, or other help oriented organizations who offer occasional, temporary relief for the caretaker. If a nursing home or adult foster care home is used, try to locate one nearby, so that you can act as an advocate. There are many decisions, sometimes daily, that need to be made on behalf of an Alzheimer's patient. Being close by allows intimate involvement in every aspect of your loved one's life, especially with decisions they can no longer make for themselves.

If you choose a nursing home or an adult foster care home, get to know the owners or caretakers. Let them know of your interest. Unable to communicate properly, the Alzheimer's victim is often defenseless concerning medication, health measures, and living conditions. They need a friendly advocate, and you may be called to that role.

9. Medical Preferences

Learn their wishes for medical treatment, including such issues as resuscitation, intubations, hospital testing, etc. This is a controversial issue, but the majority of doctors will abide by the wishes of the family. Some hospital procedures are unnecessary, yet routinely done. A good rule of thumb might be to use only tests that will lead to results that are helpful. You will need to act as their advocate in health matters as well.

If it is the wish of the patient not to be resuscitated if they have obviously died, it is imperative to already have a DNR (Do Not Resuscitate) document in place. This is covered in a Living Will. Although this issue did not become a question for my mother, it did for Bill's mother. Carmen was 95 when she passed away in her bed one evening. At the time, she was in a nursing home near us. We went right over, in hopes of having a few parting words, but by the time we arrived, she was clearly gone. She had signed a DNR order many years prior, but because it was not in the hands of the EMT (Emergency Medical Technician) when they arrived on the scene, they began to set up equipment to resuscitate her.

I ran down the hall to the nurse's station and breathlessly asked them to quickly find her DNR order in the files. We needed it immediately in her room. Fortunately, the EMT boss walked in and stalled the resusitation procedure until I arrived back with the form. It was then we learned that if the EMT does not have the written order in hand, by law in Michigan, they are required to resuscitate. Thank God, Carmen was spared that violation of her wishes. You might want to check with your loved one's wishes on this important issue and, if applicable, talk to an attorney about the laws in your state.

10. List Medications

Make a list of the medications they take and update the need for each with their doctor. You will also need that list with each new doctor they see. Upon scrutiny of Mother's medications, I found she took several she didn't need. My Medical Durable Power of Attorney gave me the right to intercede. During one hospital stay, I had to halt medications they thought she took which her doctor had eliminated months before. Unfortunately, over-medicating is a common practice among the elderly. It's important to stay on top of this issue.

When Carmen had moved to Michigan, she was taking 18 medications. Over several months, under a doctor's scrutiny, we had her pared back to five. The others had been prescribed to overcome side effects from original drugs. It can be a relentless cycle if not carefully monitored.

11. Medical and Supplemental Insurance

Be aware of the person's medical insurance, and make sure they are covered by Medicare part A and B. This includes most hospital and doctor care. Transfer Medicare payments to your address if not paid directly to the doctor. Alzheimer's patients are incapable of following up on bills.

Also check on supplemental insurance. Medicare doesn't cover everything, and a supplemental policy with a reputable company will cover most, if not all, of the remaining expenses. Remember, after Medicare pays, you may be responsible to send in the paper work to receive coverage from the supplemental insurance. Be aware of how your company handles this. Some care facilities negotiate only with Medicare.

12. Funeral Pre-Arrangements

Pre-arrange for a funeral. This sounds like a sad suggestion, but it is realistic, and you will find it helpful when the time
comes to have already taken this step. If possible, find out the
person's desire beforehand, whether they want to be buried or
cremated. Several months before Mother passed away, I visited
one of our local mortuaries. I filled out all the necessary forms,
selected a casket, and discussed the arrangements. It saved
making difficult decisions later during a more emotional time.
Mother had bought a plot in Arizona years before because she
wanted to be buried near my father. The funeral home made all
the arrangements for her burial, including her flight. All I had
to do was show up at the cemetery. It was a great relief to know
all these things were in place when the time came.

Hopefully, these twelve suggestions will help to simplify
the business end of taking over someone's life. There are many
decisions to be made when you become a caretaker/advocate.
Any way you find to streamline the process will leave more
time for you to love and nurture. I am not a lawyer, but I know
it is less expensive to plan ahead than to clean up the mess
later. Plus, with planning, the patient can be more assured of
their will being fulfilled as closely as possible to their desire.

Appendix 2
Helpful Books and Websites

Although not much was written about Alzheimer's in the early 1990's, I did find a few excellent books that were helpful.

"The 36 Hour Day," by Nancy L. Mace and Peter V. Rabins, M.D.

"Glimpses of Grace," by Rosemary J. Upton.

"When Your Loved One Has Alzheimer's," by David L. Carroll.

One thing that I did not have available during my mother's final days was help from the computer. Today, there are many good websites to go to for support and assistance. You can learn what Alzheimer's is, what symptoms to be aware of, medical issues, caretaking, and much more. I've listed four sites that I would recommend,not only for information, but for ways to get involved.

Alzheimer's Association: www.alz.org

Alzheimer's Foundation of America: www.alzfdn.org

Elder Care: www.eldercare.gov

Government Site: www.nia.nih.gov/alzheimers

Appendix 3
Symptoms and Stages of Alzheimer's

B elow I've recapped some of the common issues books and websites address. Under each area, I've entered the types of behavior I observed in Mother that seemed to fit each category. Doing this helped me see on paper a comprehensive list that identified exactly what could be observed in my mother's conduct. Perhaps you recognize these same or similar aberrations in someone you are close to. Almost everyone knows of someone who is suffering from Alzheimer's today.

1. Forgetfulness due to short term memory loss
   - Couldn't find her glasses, her purse, or keys
   - Forgot how to run the washer and other appliances
   - Unable to perform familiar tasks: dressing, turning on a shower, combing her hair
   - Couldn't balance her checkbook
   - Gave up cooking

- Forgot appointments, even when reminded
- Unable to remember her medications
- Incapable of making wise financial decisions

2. Disorientation and Confusion

- Disorientation about room locations
- Unaware of time
- Night wandering
- Became lost when driving
- Disorientation concerning distances - wanted people who lived hundreds of miles away to pick her up

3. Incontinence

4. Communication abilities waned

- Sentences drifted off
- Couldn't remember words
- Lost thoughts mid-sentence
- Interrupted conversation to read or talk aloud about things unrelated to conversation

5. Suspicion and Paranoia

- Blamed family and others for lost items
- Felt people stole from her

- Hid money, jewelry
- Delusions and hallucinations
- Thought she was pregnant
- Her image in a mirror represented "that girl," an enemy
- Thought pictures were real people and conversed with them
- Convinced that her carpet was full of bugs that crunched
- Imagined animals lived with her

6. Withdrew from social life
   - Rarely saw friends
   - Quit playing bridge and going to parties

7. Agitation and Pacing
   - Easily upset
   - Agitated about future appointments and dates
   - Paced back and forth
   - Sleep Disturbances
   - Woke up at all hours of the night
   - Diminished concept of day and night
   - Antisocial conduct
   - Going out in public not fully clothed

- Cleaned restrooms in restaurants
- Told bazaar stories to strangers

Sorting out symptoms helped me better understand Mother's disease and what to expect. I was thankful to have the research and stories of others who had walked this path before me. It helped me to see that professional people had meticulously researched, categorized, and listed common symptoms of Alzheimer's. As I read their descriptions of what Alzheimer behavior looked like, it became easier for me to accept Mother's strange behavior as her new normal.

Stages of Alzheimer's

Having named the behaviors observed in Alzheimer's, I thought it would also be helpful to categorize them into stages. When the doctor reported to me that Mother was in the moderate to severe stage of the disease, I began to review a sheet I had received at the Alzheimer's conference.[8] It outlined the three stages an Alzheimer's patient goes through. Each stage is characterized by certain behavior. With this list, I could see the progression of the disease in my mother and gain an awareness of what things to expect in the future.

The First Stage

1. Forgetfulness/memory impairment
2. Impairment in judgment
3. Increasing inability to handle routine tasks
4. Lack of spontaneity
5. Lessening of initiative
6. Disorientation of time and places
7. Depression and terror

The Second Stage:

1. Wandering and perseveration (persistent repetition)
2. Increased disorientation
3. Increased forgetfulness
4. Agitation and restlessness, especially at night
5. Inability to attach meaning to sensory perceptions
6. Inability to think abstractly
7. Muscle twitching may develop
8. Convulsive seizures possible
9. Repetitive actions

The Third Stage:

1. Increased disorientation
2. Complete dependence
3. Inability to recognize themselves in a mirror
4. Various forms of speech impairment to complete muteness
5. May develop a morbid need to put everything into their mouths
6. May develop a necessity to touch everything in sight
7. Become emaciated
8. Complete loss of control of all body functions
9. Inability to recognize people

It should be noted that the stages overlap, and not every anomaly will necessarily be seen in every Alzheimer's victim. As the disease progressed, I noticed behavior from every stage in Mother. Others have told me that their Alzheimer's relatives have also shown varying degrees of the stages. In other words, the stages don't seem to be cut and dry. They differ with individuals, but most of the symptoms seem to show up at one time or another.

With that, I end my journey, my adventure in God. May God's power and presence keep you in a place of peace as you travel your own road.

Endnotes:

1. Alzheimer's Association. 2012 Alzheimer's disease facts and figures. *Alzheimer's and Dementia: The Journal of the Alzheimer's Association.* March 2012; 8:131–168, [article online]; video available from http://www.alz.org/alzheimers_disease_facts_and_figures.asp#quickfacts; accessed February 2012.

2 "Does the Male Penguin Sit on the Egg?" *Earthsky Communications, Inc.*, (Dec. 13, 2009), [article online]; available from http://earthsky.org/biodiversity/male-penguin-eggs; accessed February 2012.

3. Phil Lindner, "Power Bible CD," Adam Clark's Commentary, Isa. 49:16, [CD-ROM], (Bronson, MO: Online Publishing, Inc., 6 January 2004).

4. Beth Moore, *James, Mercy Triumphs*, (Nashville: Lifeway Press, 2011), 43-44.

5. Elisabeth Kubler-Ross and David Kessler, "5 Stages of Grief," 2000-2012 [article online]; available from http://grief.com/the-five-stages-of-grief/; accessed 3 February 2012.

6. David L. Carroll, *When Your Loved One Has Alzheimer's*, (New York: Harper and Row, 1989), 100-117.

7. Beth Moore, *James, Mercy Triumphs*, (Nashville: Lifeway Press, 2011), 46.

8. Severience, Ruth, M.S., a Gerentological Nurse, "Alzheimer's Disease," (Independence, Missouri: Comprehensive Mental Health Services, Inc., 1989, Photocopied).

Acknowledgements

I would like to acknowledge my amazing husband, Bill, my sweet daughter, Kim Hapner, and my dear friend, Sue Werschky for their time, prayers, and help in editing my book. Your assistance was so valuable. I appreciated your suggestions and the scrutiny with which you meticulously looked over each page. I love you all dearly and couldn't have done this without you.

Author's Biography

Betsy Tacchella lives in Sturgis, Michigan with her husband of fifty years. She has three children and eight grandchildren. Betsy has been teaching the Bible for over forty years and has a Master's degree in Biblical Studies from Trinity Theological Seminary. She also mentors women and does public speaking. You may purchase her book, "Mother Has Alzheimer's" at www.xulonpress.com, www.amazon.com or www.barnesandnoble.com. You may contact the author at snowcountry02@hotmail.com. Betsy's blog is www.motherhasalzheimers.weebly.com.

CPSIA information can be obtained at www.ICGtesting.com
Printed in the USA
LVOW121524030912

297185LV00001B/157/P